Basic Investing
in Resource Stocks

The Idiot's Guide

Robert Moriarty

Also by Robert Moriarty
    Nobody Knows Anything
    The Art of Peace
    Crap Shoot
    Exposed!
    Entrapped!

First Edition

Typesetting and layout by Jeremy Irwin, jc9cz@yahoo.com

Thanks to Chris Webber for help with the charts

Library of Congress Cataloging-in-Publication Data has been applied for.

ISBN: 9781795249324

Dedication

To Trigg and Maurice who have bugged me for years to write this book. Perhaps now they will get off my back.

I made my money by selling too soon. — Bernard Baruch

Only when the last tree has died and the last river has been poisoned and the last fish been caught will we realize we cannot eat money. — Native American proverb

Wealth consists not in having great possessions, but in having few wants. — Epictetus

There are no patents in finance. — Stephen A. Schwarzman

Many have made a trade of delusions and false miracles, deceiving the stupid multitudes. — Leonardo da Vinci

An investment in knowledge pays the best interest. — Benjamin Franklin

If you don't own gold, you know neither history nor economics. — Ray Dalio

If you're not a contrarian, you're a victim. — Rick Rule

People make investing seem more difficult than it should. — Warren Buffett

In investing, what is comfortable is rarely profitable. — Robert Arnott

Always forgive your enemies. Nothing annoys them so much. — Oscar Wilde

You have enemies? Good. That means you've stood up for something, sometime in your life. — Winston Churchill

CONTENTS

List of Figures

Introduction

I fully intended to call this book *The Idiot's Guide to Investing in Resource Stocks*, but then I realized potential readers might imagine I was talking about them. It's always a good policy to wait for a paragraph or two before insulting those who might be induced into tossing a few dollars down for a good read.

I was talking about me. I'm the idiot who has made damned near every single mistake that you can possibly make when investing.

Many years ago, when I was a fledgling pilot, an older and wiser instructor whispered a few words of wisdom to me. Well, of course all the instructors were older; I was a student.

"Don't keep making the same mistake again and again. Why bother doing the identical thing when you can go and make completely new mistakes?"

He continued, "God made pencils with erasers so you could wipe out an error. But when your eraser wears out before your pencil, God is trying to tell you something."

People get it right now and again. Being human, they also make a lot of mistakes. I certainly know I did. We can read book after book about investing geniuses, but rarely do the writers discuss the dumb things they did and how they would have done things differently, had they only known better.

You don't learn anything by doing something perfectly the first time. Making mistakes and having the opportunity to change is the only way we can learn. The whole purpose of this book is to try to help the reader learn from all the errors I made.

I got back from two years in Vietnam in early 1970. I had some money saved up. I became engaged to a Donut Dollie while I was in Da Nang. She put every spare cent of her tiny income into mutual funds. She kept trying to convince me that you could do no wrong by investing in mutual funds.

I recall thinking at the time that while she was a fine looking specimen of the species, she had no background whatsoever in finance. It seemed to me that she was just following the crowd. From my vantage point it didn't seem to be working, since her funds kept going lower and lower. The Dow topped in 1966, started down and kept on going.

I got back to the world and had orders to Marine Corps Air Station El Toro in Santa Ana for the few months that remained on my tour. Since putting money into stocks was popular and seemed the right thing to do, I opened a brokerage account and prepared myself to invest.

I was smart enough to ask the broker how and when the market decline would end. I didn't want to just throw money at the market in the hopes of catching the brass ring. To his credit, the broker had looked into how markets act. He gave me good advice. He said that the market would keep going down day after day, week after week, until investors were fed up. At that point they would capitulate and dump shares at any price, just to get out. Typically the market would tumble on the Friday and plunge on Monday, and the time to invest would be about an hour after the open on Tuesday.

Further to his credit, he suggested buying options on a quality stock that had gone down a lot between Friday and Tuesday. Investors today take puts and calls for granted, but 50 years ago all options were negotiated one by one, over the counter.

We picked a stock called Great Western Finance. As I recall, the stock had been about $20 a share for a long time. In the third week of May 1970 it began a plunge that took it from $20 on the Friday to just over $12 on Tuesday, May 26. I pulled the trigger and bought six-month call options on a few hundred Great Western Finance shares.

In my very first shot at investing, the broker got it dead right. I dived in just as the market turned and surged higher. It was so easy to make money in the stock market.

The day you start thinking you are smarter than the market, you have made a giant mistake that will cost you dearly. When it looks really easy it is at its most dangerous. I realized that the broker had given me valuable information and I began to trust him for good advice.

While the calls had many months left on them before expiry, I was smart enough to understand that my purpose in investing was to make money. I sold at a 200 percent profit a couple of weeks after entering the trade.

I committed two giant mistakes. Since I had made a lot of money in a short time, I thought investing was easy and I trusted the broker. It took me years and lots of money to learn that both were serious errors in judgment.

My sincere hope is that by sharing my regular acts of stupidity with you, you might be spared the same expense. Someone has to pay for every mistake in one form or another, and it will be a lot cheaper for you if you listen as I explain how foolish I have been.

Chapter 1
State of the Financial Union

ON AUGUST 15, 1971, President Richard Nixon broke gold's last tie to the world's financial system. The dollar went from being as good as gold to being as good as paper, literally overnight. Since that time governments of all sorts have engaged in a frenzy of printing and spending money they didn't have. It was as if Nixon granted the world an unlimited supply of paper and ink and told them it was possible to print wealth out of thin air.

To spend now reduces our ability to make future purchases. Borrowing in order to spend now does nothing more than bring consumption forward and lays a burden of debt on future generations. True prosperity never comes from consumption but rather from saving for an unknowable future. When you have already spent your own future, it's foolish. When you have spent the futures of your children and grandchildren, it's criminal. Thomas Jefferson said, "It is incumbent on every generation to pay its own debts as it goes."

In the developed world today, when children are born the government handcuffs them with a debt burden they may never shed. Governments of all sizes and colors are forcing investors into making an important decision about their future. Each of us must decide. Do you want to be rich or do you want to be poor?

Stable civilizations are best measured by the size of their middle class. Every society has had rich and has had poor. That has been true forever, no matter where the country was located, or when. But as overall wealth grew, primarily due to the benefit of easy use of money and eventually nearly free energy, civilization grew and spread. But it remains accurate to say some will always be poor and others will always be wealthy. What matters most is the stability of government, and that mostly depends on the size of the middle class.

When governments declare war on the middle class, they are declaring war on themselves. Eventually the newly poor begin to envy the newly rich, and a revolution begins.

In any normal, rational time, investing in resource stocks would be the act of a gambler who hones his skills on the craps tables in Vegas and buys a handful of cheap lottery tickets on the way home from the bar in the faint hope of collecting a multimillion-dollar payoff.

It's been my experience that resource companies are often run by idiots pretending to be managers who live the good life while sucking the financial blood out of the veins of helpless investors. It's a dangerous business, where failure is the norm. Share prices run up and down faster than a bride's nightie. I've run into charlatans, con men and fools. I've visited hundreds of mining properties and I've been lied to on almost every trip.

I find that wonderful, being lied to maybe 75 percent of the time. I used to be in the computer business. There I got lied to 100 percent of the time. So the liars in mining are at best amateurs in comparison.

But these are not rational or normal times, and investing in resource shares may be the only logical investment for those looking to hedge other potentially more dangerous alternatives. Remember, it was only a little over a year ago that every punter and his grandmother were tossing pesos into what I call the Bitcon pool. I passed on the whole madness, seeing it as nothing more than a variation of an electronic Beanie Baby.

At one point in late 2017 the total value of the 1,300 varieties of Bitcon amounted to over $800 billion. As of January 2019 the number of Bitcon look-alikes is up to 2,533 but the combined net worth of all of them is down to $136,368,981,000, roughly.

That means $663 billion flew off to Bitcon heaven. We were told to buy Bitcon in all its varieties because it was limited in supply. Nothing with 2,533 variations is limited or rare.

The United States Federal Government is adding to the national debt at a rate unparalleled in history. One day very soon those 2,533 variations of Bitcon may well seem a lot more logical than the debt of the US government.

When you look up and see what seems to be a layer of dark and foreboding clouds, it may well be nothing more than a bevy or wedge of black swans. No one can say just which black swan will land first, but it's an easy prediction that with so many black swans circling, at least one is bound to be wheels-down soon. When that happens, The Great Reset begins.

Chapter 2
The Great Reset

I READ THAT the total debt in the world today is in the neighborhood of $250 trillion. To me, and I suspect to most readers, the number is so large as to be meaningless. To put it in better perspective, we could perhaps compare it to the world's yearly production of goods and services, estimated to be in the vicinity of $90 trillion. Now those two figures do not provide a complete picture, only a relative number.

Let's use two smaller numbers, but with the same ratio. If you owe $35,000 but have an income of $12,600 a year, you have a debt problem. Now multiply that by every person on earth: young, old, infirm, all of the 7.7 billion breathing today. The level of debt in many countries is higher than at any point in history. We know that countries go broke regularly and always have done.

That's in an environment of zero or negative interest rates. Now that becomes insane. If corporations and governments can't maintain a reasonable balance between income and outgo with negative interest rates, just how do they expect to cope with normal historic interest rates?

When I was going to college in the early 1970s, I majored in economics. I was at both Columbia in New York City and Iona College in New Rochelle. I worked all day and attended night school. Being in and around New York City, both schools attracted top-notch economics professors from Wall Street. I learned a lot — mostly to ignore conventional economics and Keynesian theory.

If I would have submitted a paper even suggesting the possibility of negative interest rates, I not only would have flunked the course, I would have been ejected from the classroom.

"Negative interest rates, you say? Have you lost your cotton-picking mind? Out!"

"Now! Out! Get out of my classroom, you moron."

Today you can read every day about what a great idea it is to loan money to governments that guarantee you will receive less in return. That's quite goofy.

If you get nothing else from this book, learn at least one important element. It will justify the couple of bucks you may have plunked down for the sucker.

All debts get paid.

I will repeat myself because it's such a vital element to understanding finance and investing.

ALL DEBTS GET PAID.

They are paid either by the borrower or by the lender.

I remember loaning a fellow some money while we were playing craps in the O-Club in Meridian, Mississippi, one Friday night happy hour in 1966. That's already one serious mistake on my part, you are no doubt thinking.

Playing craps wasn't a mistake. I have made a heap of money over the years shooting dice, starting on my first night in boot camp in San Diego in 1964, using a set of dice made from chalk. I suspect our young men and women undergoing the same rite of passage today probably forgo shooting dice, and that's a pity. In combat and in investing, understanding the odds of every roll is vital.

In short, if you want to know how to invest at a profit, knowing the odds helps a lot.

Back to the O-Club in Meridian. My first loan ever was never repaid by the borrower. Eventually it sunk in that if he wasn't going to pay, then what I believed to be an asset wasn't. So I ended up paying, to my great surprise.

All debts get paid. If not by the borrower, then by the lender. Alas, we are told that if the US government goes into debt to the tune of over $1 trillion a year, most of it is owed to ourselves so it really doesn't matter. It's not as if we owe it to another country.

That's really dumb thinking.

Here's why.

The US Treasury releases a financial statement each year. The 2016 statement showed that the US government's 75-year unfunded liability just for Social Security and Medicare totaled $46.7 trillion. That's money that we "owe to ourselves," so a lot of writers suggest we ignore it. It's not as if it's a real debt.

Well, if you are planning on collecting Social Security or using Medicare 25 years from now, the government not paying its debts means no money for you. So if the government doesn't pay its debt, you get to pay it instead, by forgoing Social Security or Medicare.

Have fun in your retirement years without the income or insurance that you were promised. Do let me know how you feel about debts to you not being paid, and if you think it's important or not.

Professor Laurence Kotlikoff from Boston University suggests the total unfunded liability of the United States government is really more like $210 trillion. He came up with that number in 2015. It's a lot higher today.

The fact is that virtually every government in the world today is functionally insolvent as a result of buying votes from the populace by making a series of financial promises that it cannot possibly keep.

That's what the Yellow Vests revolution in France is all about. That has spread to Taiwan, Israel, Jordan, Lebanon, the Netherlands, Egypt, China, and even Brussels, home to Europe's greatest stupidity in government.

It's something I predicted in a book I published three years ago, titled *The Art of Peace*. In the book I suggested that all empires end when they begin to engage in military adventurism. That is to say, wars that you don't need to fight. You just feel like showing off your strength, like a 14-year-old boy riding a bicycle on one wheel to impress a 14-year-old girl. It may look cool but you don't really need to do it.

Anyone who has thought at all about it can see that of the various wars the US has engaged in since September 11, 2001, none of them has accomplished anything.

Anything worth doing is worth doing right. Anything not worth doing is not worth doing.

They have cost a lot of money, as yet unpaid, and have destroyed any good opinion the rest of the world may have had of the US as the home of the brave and land of the free. How about the land of the enslaved and hopelessly bankrupt?

I said in my book that the world was awash in debt that could never be repaid. The result would be the first worldwide revolution.

Rumblings from the masses have been going on for almost a year but became visible only when protestors in France, wearing the yellow vests or *gilets jaunes* that are required to be kept in every vehicle, began to demonstrate all over France in November of 2018.

I'll say more on the Yellow Vests in a later chapter since they are so important to what is happening today.

No one ever wants to address the real issue. Just who is going to pay for the cradle-to-grave benefits all these governments have promised? The arithmetic doesn't work.

Those folks in France know how to run a revolution about as well as they understand how a guillotine functions.

Just as a small matter of interest, one of the causes of the French Revolution of 1789 was the government getting involved in the American Revolution and bankrupting itself in the process, fighting a war that did nothing for France. Those running governments around the world today should think about how their heads would look on the end of a pike. It's happened before.

I read a piece just today about a survey recently taken in Ireland by the European Broadcasting Union's *Generation What?* research group. Questions were asked of 20,000 people about their attitudes toward various groups. A full 36 percent of them viewed politicians as corrupt and an additional 40 per cent believed they were partly corrupt.

In the 18–34 age group an incredible 54 per cent added that they would take part in a "large scale uprising against the generation in power if it happened in the next days or months."

By and large, the Gilets Jaunes protests have been a mishmash of calm protestors angry at a system that ignores their problems and needs. There are no leaders. There is no single agenda. It's just a mix of protestors spread over the whole of France. Almost all the violence comes from the police.

Yellow Vests walking in Oloron, France. *(Robert Moriarty)*

I spent a couple of months in Switzerland writing my last two books. When you ask the Swiss how their government works, they tend to get that "deer in the headlights" look. They know what you are asking; they just don't know how to answer.

The government in Switzerland works by working. The president of the country has an entirely titular position, his biggest role being to preside over the Swiss Guards — who aren't in Switzerland anyway, as they guard the Pope in Rome.

If you reside in Switzerland and you have a really great idea, or even a really daft idea, if you can convince eight cantons or 50,000 voters to support your concept, the country will hold a binding referendum on the matter.

A couple of years ago someone wanted to test the concept of a guaranteed basic income. Now that sounds at first like a wonderful idea: no working, free money. They got the signatures, a referendum was held, and the idea was promptly killed. It was Switzerland after all, and they know a daft idea when they hear it.

I sense that throughout the world, ordinary people feel hopeless in the face of big government. Major organizations have undertaken studies and concluded that in the US, voting doesn't change anything. It's a waste of time, a sop thrown to the masses to make them feel they have a voice. But people aren't stupid and they know they don't have a voice. For years, most Americans have supported withdrawal from Iraq and Afghanistan but no one in Washington listens.

With the coming of the Internet, people begin to realize we don't really need big government. Politicians have always been prostitutes. They sell their souls for votes, but once in power all they do is line their own pockets and the pockets of those special interest groups who launched them into office.

Governance in the world today simply and clearly doesn't work. It doesn't represent the will of ordinary people and it needs changing. We are entering what I believe will be the time of the greatest financial disaster in world history. As we do, ordinary people across the entire world are beginning to demand both change and representation. The Gilets Jaunes movement is merely the opening round, not the end. It's not only not the end, it's not even the end of the beginning.

The banking system went on life support back in September of 2008. As bad as banks have been historically, since 2008 they have resembled nothing less than casinos run by the Mafia. Some banks, such as Wells Fargo, have been smacked with billions of dollars in fines for clearly stealing from their customers. In reality the fines are nothing more than a tax on fraud on the part of the US federal government. Certainly the customers who were defrauded by Wells Fargo didn't get one cent of their money back.

The perennial bad boy of European banking, Deutsche Bank, maintains a notional derivatives book of $46 trillion, or 12 percent of the entire world's derivatives exposure. We are told the figure is meaningless because the net exposure is far less than the notional value, but those saying that have skipped an important part of the issue.

The magic behind derivatives is a theory that you reduce risk by spreading it out. Actually you do the opposite; you multiply risk because you have introduced counter-party risk. Here's how I explain counter-party risk, and why it increases at a geometric rate as size increases.

Imagine yourself as someone controlling trillions in oil wealth. You control a seemingly endless flow of cash and if someone pisses you off, you can whack them and expect to get away with it.

You walk into any casino in Vegas and go up to the craps table. You ask the dealer if you can make a million-dollar bet on one roll of the dice. He agrees. When you make the bet, one of two things will happen. You either win and get $1 million, or you lose and fork over a lot of $100 bills. You are so rich that you really don't care.

But you like action, so you go to the biggest-grossing casino in the world, in

Macau. But now you want to make a billion-dollar bet. That's a big bet, so the floor boss has to check with the main office, but he takes the bet with a smile. Once again, at that point you can either win or lose. If the dice favor you, you walk out with a check for a billion dollars. If they don't, you hand over another, far bigger pile of $100 bills.

Since that worked out so well, you ask the casino manager if he can make one more bet, this time for $1 trillion. This time the manager just smiles a broad smile and nods. He doesn't have to ask anyone for permission. He really likes this bet.

At that point only one thing can happen.

You can only lose.

It doesn't matter a rat's ass what the dice do; there isn't a casino in the entire world that can cover a trillion-dollar loss. The casino manager knew it the whole time and didn't care. If you crap out, the casino is rich beyond their wildest imagination. If you roll a seven or an eleven on the first roll, the casino can't pay anyway so they don't care.

It wasn't the nature of the bet that made it a good or bad bet; it was the size. And at some point as derivatives increase in size, you are no longer just incurring a financial risk but adding counter-party risk.

With Deutsche Bank holding $46 trillion in derivatives, when a systemic crash begins, the meaningless notional exposure may well become a very real net exposure. Let me give you another example, because frankly I suspect there are only three people in the entire world who actually fully understand derivatives and two of them are a bit confused.

You look at Deutsche Bank and read that its stock price has dropped by 80 percent in the last five years. Due to loan losses and built-in losses in its derivatives book, the bank is headed for the rubbish pile. If and when Deutsche Bank collapses, that particular rolling snowball is going to become the mother of all avalanches by the time it reaches the valley floor, sweeping every other bank in the world along with it.

You realize that's a really bad thing to happen. The Dow and S&P might drop 20 percent in a day and gold might go up by $500 an ounce in a day. The S&P is trading at 2570 and gold is at $1,285. You buy puts on the S&P at 2100 because they sell for pennies. That way, should you be right and the entire system blows up, you have incredible leverage. Likewise, you buy calls on gold at $1,600 for exactly the same reason. They too sell for pennies.

Sounds like a good deal, right? Let's say the unthinkable then happens and the stock market does plummet, taking the S&P to 1800. Gold goes to $2,000 an ounce as it is the last man standing.

At this point you need to think about how rich you just became. I can actually work it out in my head, it is so easy. You just lost everything you put into the puts and calls.

Those gold calls that sold for pennies are in theory worth $40,000 apiece. The S&P puts work out to $30,000 each. But your counter-party, no matter who it was, is broke. Counter-party risk kicked in as a result of the size of the movement in prices. And no one is going to bail them out this time. There isn't enough money in the world unless the US goes into the Monopoly money business. Which is certainly an option.

The world's financial system came within hours of collapse in September of 2008 because of what seemed to be some relatively meaningless derivatives. But when notional value morphs into actual value, the game is over. 2008 was just the opening round of the collapse of the world's financial system. We are moving rapidly into the most dangerous part of the crash.

The London office of AIG was playing fast and loose with credit default swaps on sub-prime mortgages. As an example, a tiny hedge fund similar in nature to AIG insured UBS for $1.3 billion of sub-prime mortgages for a premium of $2 million a year. As long as the mortgages didn't default, the hedge fund was raking in the dough and making an annualized return of 44 percent. Then, in 2007, mortgages began to be defaulted upon. UBS called in its insurance claim and the hedge fund refused to pay. So UBS made an insurance claim. It didn't get paid, and found it was now on the hook for $1.3 billion. It didn't get its $2 million back either.

The London office of AIG literally put the entire company at risk by doing the same thing on a far larger scale. In their minds, they were privatizing financial gains and counting on the government to bail them out in the event of losses. The US government did bail out AIG, to the tune of $85 billion.

While the full figure may never be known, the US Treasury was handing out bundles of $100 bills to every bank in the world like candy to kids on Halloween. The total cost was in the trillions of dollars, all borrowed. The actions of the central banks did nothing more than convince the banks that the government would always be there to save them.

But maybe not. Things continue right up to the point where they stop.

The world is awash in debt that no one actually believes will be paid; the middle-class is being crushed between the rock of higher taxes and the hard place of constant inflation. And they have had enough. All over the world, protests are growing daily. They will continue to grow until the system blows up. Then we have The Great Reset, where we return to a level of government the middle class can afford.

If you think about it, it's very simple. There is only a certain level of government any country can afford. Once you go above that level you are asking for problems and are guaranteed to get them.

Now this may sound irrational because you aren't hearing it from anyone else, but the only solution is to cut back on government until it returns to a level you can afford. There are no other options; you can't print your way out and you can't borrow your way out. You have to reduce government.

There are some actions you can take to protect yourself. That's what this whole book is about.

Chapter 3
Moriarty's Dozen Rules of Investing

1. All markets are manipulated all of the time by everybody involved. If you can't handle that, don't invest.

2. Markets go up, markets go down.

3. Markets tend to overshoot, and when they do, there is often an equal and opposite move.

4. With any investment, buy cheap and sell expensive.

5. Markets deviate from the mean and always regress to the mean.

6. The most dangerous words in investing are "This time it's different." It's never different.

7. Weak hands buy at tops and sell at bottoms. Strong hands buy at bottoms and sell at tops. It's vital that investors remember that at every top there are 50 reasons to buy, and at every bottom there are 50 reasons to sell. That's what makes them tops and bottoms.

8. In matters financial, everyone has a bias and an agenda.

9. To make money, figure out what the experts and gurus recommend and then do the opposite. For there are no true experts or gurus; only people who want others to believe they are.

10. In a bull market, pretty much everything goes up regardless of value. In a bear market, pretty much everything goes down no matter the merits of the investment. You need to know which you are in. It's not rocket science.

11. If you don't sell at a profit, the only alternative is to sell at a loss.

12. Profitable investing is simple but not easy.

Chapter 4
Why Gold? Why Now?

PEOPLE HAVE VIEWED GOLD as the ultimate store of value for most of the last 5,000 years. Gold formed part and parcel of money right up until 2000, when the Swiss franc became the last currency to sever its tie to gold. As long ago as 3100 B.C. the Egyptians assessed gold as being worth 2.5 times as much as the same weight of silver. Now it's about 85 times more valuable.

Gold vs Silver

6 Month	2 Year	5 Year	10 Year	20 Year	Long Term

Gold v Silver

world gold charts © www.goldchartsrus.com

Figure 1. Gold–silver spread, August 2018 to January 2019.

Much of the first part of the book is about current events because if I am correct, we are starting the most significant financial collapse in all of world history. What I write about investing will stay current no matter when the reader reads this book. But I'm hesitant to go into depth about many of the resources because in the greatest depression the world has ever seen, protecting what you have will be far more important than speculating on commodity resources. So it's both a bit of a history book and a finance book at the same time. I can only hope investors will be patient with me.

As I will go into in later chapters, all investments move from one absurd extreme to the other, either overbought or oversold, and most often overshoot. For many centuries, gold was money. For the last 40 years gold hasn't been money, but as people begin to understand the real intrinsic value of paper and of government promises, attitudes will change. Pieces of paper have no more intrinsic value than do any other promises from government.

I see gold as a solution to our continuing financial chaos. It worked for much of history and nothing says it won't work again.

Figure 2. Gold–silver spread, 1999–2019.

Gold isn't a religion. You should avoid those preaching that you must worship at the Church of the Holy Gold. Much of the time it's an investment. It may again be the best form of money, but most of all it is a hedge against government stupidity and financial calamity and a wonderful insurance policy.

If you don't own some gold (or silver or platinum or palladium or rhodium) that you can lay your hands on, you may regret it. Precious metals are the most secure insurance policy that you can buy to protect your financial house, even as it begins to burn down.

Young people today seem to think that their most important job is to save the world. Screw saving the world. Save your family and yourself by taking out the planet's oldest and most dependable insurance plan.

While I will be talking about investing in other precious metals later in the book, for now, consider all the precious metals as being similar enough in nature that if you invest in any of the five — gold, silver, platinum, rhodium and palladium — you are still buying an insurance policy first and an investment second.

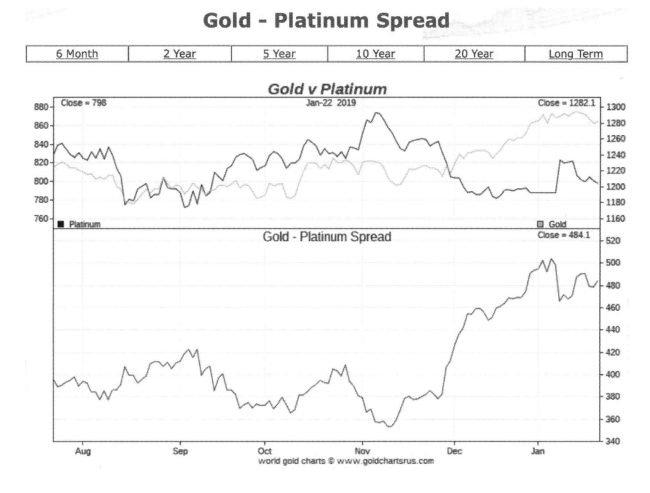

Figure 3. Gold–platinum spread, Aug 2018 to Jan 2019.

Lately I have actually been selling gold and putting the money into both silver and platinum. Figures 1 to 4 in this Chapter 4 will show you why.

As I write, early in 2019, it takes a little over 84 ounces of silver to purchase one ounce of gold. You always want to buy what is cheap and sell what is dear. The gold to silver ratio has been as high as 86:1 in the last month. So, ignoring where you believe the metals will go in price, in relative terms silver is cheap compared to gold.

The ratio has varied from 17:1 to 100:1 over the past 100 years; the mean average is 53:1. Silver has spent less than one percent of that time above 85:1, so by buying silver and selling gold now, you are entering a trade that has been profitable for 99 percent of the last 100 years.

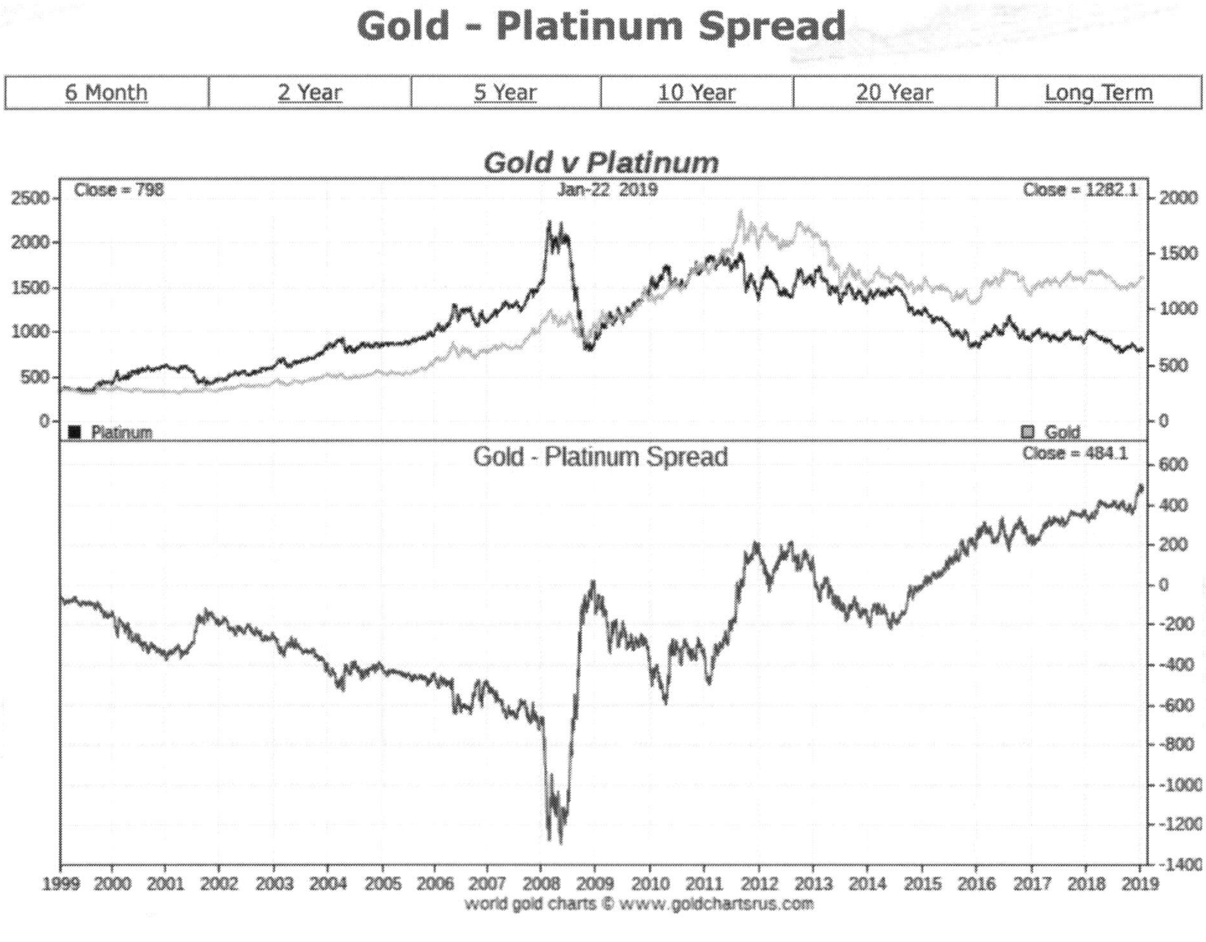

Gold - Platinum Spread

| 6 Month | 2 Year | 5 Year | 10 Year | 20 Year | Long Term |

Figure 4. Gold–platinum spread, 1999–2019.

Likewise, platinum reached a discount to gold of just over $500 an ounce in January 2019. That has never happened before in all of the time platinum has been trading. I track it closely and I watched in wonder as the spread between gold and platinum went from a $350 discount to a $501 discount in about eight weeks.

Take my word; nothing has changed in the fundamentals. There has been no news that would justify such a major move. Relative to gold, platinum is incredibly cheap and we will almost certainly see a snap back move.

All commodities deviate from the mean at times, and always regress to the mean. Prices naturally go up and naturally go down, but they always go back to the mean eventually. It's the nature of markets; nothing goes straight up or straight down or even straight. Markets zig and zag constantly.

Chapter 5
Don't Do What Experts Say. Never, Ever

BY EARLY 2011, the prices of gold and silver had been climbing for an entire decade. Before peaking in April of 2011, silver made one of the largest moves in commodity history, blasting from $4.01 in late November of 2001 to $49.80 on April 25, 2011. Gold went from $252.10 on August 25, 1999 to $1,921.41 in early September of 2011.

If you listened to the experts, those who supposedly know the most about precious metals, and did what they said, you would have lost your shirt. On the next few pages I reproduce an article (see the Appendix for details) published on October 27, 2011, seven weeks after the price of gold had peaked. Here is what 148 experts said at that time.

⌘ ⌘ ⌘

Is Gold On Its Way to $3,000, $5,000, $10,000 or Even Higher? These Analysts Think So

140 analysts maintain that gold will eventually reach a parabolic peak price of at least $3,000/ozt, before the bubble bursts of which 100 see gold reaching at least $5,000/ozt. 17 predict a parabolic peak price of as much as $10,000 per troy ounce of which 12 are on record as saying gold could go even higher than that. Take a look here at who is projecting what, by when and why.

12 Analysts See Gold Price Going to +$10,000
1. *DoctoRX: $20,000 (by 2020)*
2. *Mike Maloney: $15,000*
3. *Ben Davies: $10,000–$15,000*
4. *Howard Katz: $14,000*
5. *Jeffrey Lewis: $7,000–$14,000*
6. *Jim Sinclair: $12,455*
7. *Gold runner: $10,000–$12,000*
8. *Martin Armstrong: $5,000–$12,000 (by 2015–16)*
9. *Robin Griffiths: $3,000–$12,000 (by 2015)*
10. *Jim Rickards: $4,000–$11,000*
11. *Roland Watson: $10,800*
12. *Dylan Grice: $10,167*

51 Analysts See Gold Price Going Over $5,000 to as High as $10,000

1. Arnold Bock: $10,000
2. Porter Stanberry: $10,000
3. Peter George: $10,000 (by 2015)
4. Nick Barisheff: $10,000 (by 2016)
5. Tom Fischer: $10,000
6. Shayne McGuire: $10,000
7. Eric Hommelberg: $10,000
8. Marc Faber: $6,000–$10,000
9. David Petch: $6,000–$10,000
10. Gerald Celente: $6,000–$10,000
11. Egon von Greyerz: $6,000–$10,000
12. Peter Schiff: $5,000–$10,000 (in 5 to 10 years)
13. Peter Millar: $5,000–$10,000
14. Ron Paul: $5,000–$10,000
15. Roger Wiegand: $5,000–$10,000
16. Alf Field: $4,250–$10,000
17. Jeff Nielson: $3,000–$10,000
18. Dennis van Ek: $9,000 (by 2015)
19. Dominic Frisby: $8,000
20. Paul Brodsky: $8,000
21. James Turk: $8,000 (by 2015)
22. Joseph Russo: $7,000–$8,000
23. Bob Chapman: $7,700
24. Tim Guinness: $7,500 (by 2025)
25. Michael Rozeff: $2,865–$7,151
26. Jim Willie: $7,000
27. Greg McCoach: $6,500
28. Chris Mack: $6,241.64 (by 2015)
29. Chuck DiFalco: $6,214 (by 2018)
30. Jeff Clark: $6,214
31. Urs Gmuer: $6,200
32. Aubie Baltin: $6,200 (by 2017)
33. Murray Sabrin: $6,153
34. Adam Hamilton: $6,000+
35. Samuel "Bud" Kress: $6,000 (by 2014)
36. Robert Kientz: $6,000
37. Harry Schultz: $6,000
38. John Bougearel: $6,000

39. *David Tice: $5,000–$6,000*
40. *Laurence Hunt: $5,000–$6,000 (by 2019)*
41. *Taran Marwah: $6,000+*
42. *Rob Lutts: $3,000–$6,000*
43. *Martin Hutchinson: $3,100–$5,700*
44. *Stephen Leeb: $5,500 (by 2015)*
45. *Louise Yamada: $5,200*
46. *Jeremy Charlesworth: $5,000+*
47. *Przemyslaw Radomski: $5,000+*
48. *Jason Hamlin: $5,000+*
49. *David McAlvany: $5,000+*
50. *Pat Gorman: $5,000+*
51. *Mark Leibovit: $3,600–$5,000+*

Cumulative sub-total: 63

37 Analysts Believe Gold Price Could Go As High As $5,000
1. *David Rosenberg: $5,000*
2. *James West: $5,000*
3. *Doug Casey: $5,000*
4. *Peter Cooper: $5,000*
5. *Robert McEwen: $5,000 (by 2012–2014)*
6. *Peter Krauth: $5,000*
7. *Tim Iacono: $5,000 (by 2017)*
8. *Christopher Wyke: $5,000*
9. *Frank Barbera: $5,000*
10. *John Lee: $5,000*
11. *Barry Dawes: $5,000;*
12. *Bob Lenzer: $5,000 (by 2015)*
13. *Steve Betts: $5,000*
14. *Stewart Thomson: $5,000*
15. *Charles Morris: $5,000 (by 2015)*
16. *George Maniere: $5,000 (by 2015)*
17. *Marvin Clark: $5,000 (by 2015)*
18. *Eric Sprott: $5,000*
19. *Nathan Narusis: $5,000*
20. *David McAlvany: $5,000*
21. *Standard Chartered: $5,000 (by 2020)*
22. *Bud Conrad: $4,000–$5,000*

23. Paul Mylchreest: $4,000–$5,000
24. Pierre Lassonde: $4,000–$5,000
25. Willem Middelkoop: $4,000–$5,000
26. James Dines: $3,000–$5,000
27. Bill Murphy: $3,000–$5,000
28. Bill Bonner: $3,000–$5,000
29. Peter Degraaf: $2,500–$5,000
30. Eric Janszen: $2,500–$5,000
31. Larry Jeddeloh: $2,300–$5,000 (by 2013)
32. Larry Edelson: $2,300–$5,000 (by 2015)
33. Luke Burgess: $2,000–$5,000
34. Robert Lloyd-George: $5,000 (by 2014)
35. Heath Jansen: $2,500–$5,000
36. Jeff Nichols: $2,000–$5,000
37. Julian Jessop: $1,840–$5,000

Cumulative sub-total: 100

40 Analysts Believe Gold Will Increase to Between $3,000 and $4,999
1. David Moenning: $4,525
2. Larry Reaugh: $4,000+
3. Oliver Velez: $4,000+
4. Ernest Kepper: $4,000
5. Mike Knowles: $4,000
6. Ian Gordon/Christopher Funston: $4,000
7. Barry Elias: $4,000 (by 2020)
8. Lindsey Williams: $3,000–$4,000
9. Jay Taylor: $3,000–$4,000
10. Christian Barnard: $2,500–$4,000
11. John Paulson: $2,400–$4,000
12. Paul Tustain: $3,844
13. Myles Zyblock: $3,800
14. Eric Roseman: $2,500–$3,500 (by 2015)
15. Christopher Wood: $3,360
16. Peter Leeds: $3,200
17. Franklin Sanders: $3,130
18. John Henderson: $3,000+ (by 2015–17)
19. Michael Berry: $3,000+ (by 2015)
20. Hans Goetti: $3,000

21. *Michael Yorba: $3,000*
22. *David Urban; $3,000*
23. *Mitchell Langbert: $3,000*
24. *Brett Arends: $3,000*
25. *Ambrose Evans-Pritchard: $3,000*
26. *John Williams: $3,000*
27. *Byron King: $3,000*
28. *Chris Weber: $3,000 (by 2020)*
29. *Mark O'Byrne: $3,000*
30. *Kevin Kerr: $3,000*
31. *Frank Holmes: $3,000*
32. *Shamik Bhose: $3,000 (by 2014)*
33. *Ani Markova: $3,000 (by 2013/14)*
34. *John Embry: $3,000*
35. *Michael Lombardi: $3,000*
36. *Eric Bolling: $3,000*
37. *Phillip Richards: $3,000*
38. *John Ing: $3,000*
39. *Chris Laird: $3,000*
40. *Michael Brush: $3,000*

Cumulative sub-total: 140

8 Analysts Believe Price of Gold Will Go to Between $2,500 and $3,000
1. *Kurtis Hemmerling: $2,500–$3,000*
2. *Ian McAvity: $2,500–$3,000*
3. *Mary Anne and Pamela Aden: $2,000–$3,000*
4. *Graham French: $2,000–$3,000*
5. *Bank of America Merrill Lynch: $2,000–$3,000*
6. *Joe Foster: $2,000–$3,000 (by 2019)*
7. *David Morgan: $2,900*
8. *Sascha Opel: $2,500+*

Grand Total: 148

Conclusion: There you have it. Who would have believed that 148 analysts would maintain that gold and by implication, silver, are likely to achieve such lofty levels as a result of the effects of our current financially troubled and volatile times? Their rationale is varied but each is sound in its own right.

If we are to put any credence whatsoever into the rationale presented by the above analysts then it seems prudent to seriously consider owning some physical gold and silver and/or the stocks and/or long-term warrants of those companies that mine these precious metals.

Lorimer Wilson, editor of www.munKNEE.com (Your Key to Making Money!) and www.FinancialArticleSummariesToday.com (A site for sore eyes and inquisitive minds) has identified the analysts by name with their price projections and time frame. Please note that this complete paragraph, and a link back to the original article, must be included in any article posting or re-posting to avoid copyright infringement.

⌘ ⌘ ⌘

Those 148 writers and commentators would be considered the top experts in the gold business. Each had an opinion on where the price of gold was going. Actually the article did nothing more than expand on another piece on the same website in January of 2011, eight months before gold topped. On January 24, however, the author had listed only 113 "experts."

You would have to be pretty knowledgeable to figure out that there was one gold writer not on the list of experts. That would be me.

It wasn't because I wasn't asked for my opinion. I was, on both occasions. My response was the same each time. I chose not to predict a price for gold over any timeframe. Hell, I don't know what the price will be tomorrow. How on earth could I make a reasonable SWAG (Stupid, Wild-Assed Guess) as to the price in a month or year or any other time?

I don't know anyone who can do that consistently. I'd like to be known and remembered for realizing what I don't know. And I never predict price on anything. I'm not smart enough.

I can look at the price of gold and figure out if it is cheap relative to, say, silver or platinum, but I would be hopeless at guessing a future price. I believe gold will play a part in a solution to the incredible financial crisis we are entering but I can't say what the price might be. I don't think anyone can.

I suppose I should put a plug in here for a book I wrote titled *Nobody Knows Anything* and subtitled *Learn to Ignore the Experts, the Gurus and other Fools.*

I wrote it almost three years ago. It was the number one best seller in its category on Amazon for a short time. I still make sales daily. The book is available on the Apple iTunes store and Amazon in both paper and electronic formats, and in audio for the really lazy.

I go into the theory of contrarian investing in the book and it is a good companion to this book. Please buy it. If I sell ten books a day it brings in three bucks a book. I can then spring for lunch at MacDonald's and a Coffee Latte at Starbucks on the way home. It would be a giant boost to my income and I could use the money.

Just kidding. If someone understands the market well enough to show others how they really can make money, he shouldn't need to hustle for lunch money. I sell the book as cheap as I can so everyone can afford it, not to make money.

In the grinding crashes that regularly take place, no matter what the commodity, there will be "gurus," including some of the best known and most respected people in the business, explaining how that commodity will go still lower. Robert Prechter of Elliott Wave fame predicted that gold would continue dropping to $200 an ounce in 1999–2001 before hitting a long-term bottom. Martin Armstrong of Armstrong Economics also predicted gold would go below $200 an ounce.

Likewise, at tops the "gurus" see no end to the climb. Here is what John McAfee of McAfee Anti-Virus fame had to say, the week before Bitcon peaked in mid-December of 2017: *"Bubbles are mathematically impossible in this new paradigm. Gold is laughable compared to crypto currencies. How do you fractionalize gold? How do you ship it? It's physical so how do you safely store it? It was good for people 3,000 years ago. Today it is inherently worthless. Soon it will drop in value as crypto currencies climb."*

Well! So much for that call on his part. As to fractionalizing gold, I have ten Royal Mint one-gram gold coins safely stored under my bed. That's pretty fractional. If someone breaks in and tries to steal them, I dread what will happen when they wake Barbara up.

John may not have seen the bubble forming but I'll bet the crash woke his ass up. What he failed to mention, and what the SEC needed to point out to him to refresh his memory, was that he was getting $110,000 every time he pimped Bitcon on Twitter. That's a good gig if you can get it.

In the weeks and months leading up to the top in silver in April of 2011, Eric Sprott was traveling all over the world pointing out the merits of his new silver ETF. As the ETF peaked at a 25 percent premium to the price of silver, he was selling his own shares and buying physical at a guaranteed 25 percent profit.

You can't buy the past, only the future, and it's unknowable to us mere mortals.

By now you may be feeling that I am trying to tell my readers to ignore the experts. You couldn't be more mistaken.

You shouldn't do as they say, because they always get it wrong. But you must listen carefully to what the experts say. And then do the opposite.

You don't have to know anything about any investment in order to make money, other than having the ability to measure the sentiment.

Let me give you another example, this one more recent.

WALL STREET YEAR-END 2018 TARGETS FOR S&P 500

Strategist	Firm	S&P 500 Target	% Above 2017 Close
Mike Wilson	Morgan Stanley	2750	2.86%
David Kostin	Goldman Sachs	2850	6.60%
Savita Subramanian	BofA Merrill Lynch	2800	4.73%
Tony Dwyer	Canaccord	2800	4.73%
Tobia Levkovic	Citi	2675	0.05%
Dennis DeBusschere	Evercore ISI	3000	12.21%
Brian Belski	BMO Capital Markets	2950	10.34%
Binky Chada	Deutsche Bank	2850	6.60%
Keith Parker	UBS	2900	8.47%
Jonathan Golub	RBC Capital Markets	2875	7.53%
Barry Banister	Stifel Nichlaus	2750	2.86%
as of 12/31/17	**Median Target**	2850	6.60%
	Actual	2506.85	-6.24%

Figure 5. Wall Street's year-end 2018 targets for the S&P 500.

Figure 5 is taken from an article posted on January 4, 2019 on a website named Real Investment Advice (see the Appendix). The company's head strategist, Lance Roberts, wrote it and called it *The Problem With Wall Street's Forecasts*.

He began: "Over the last few weeks, I have been asked repeatedly to publish my best guess as to where the market will wind up by the end of 2019.

"Here it is: *'I don't know.'*

"The reality is that we cannot predict the future. If it were actually possible, fortunetellers would all win the lottery. They don't, we can't, and we aren't going to try."

So if the experts are always wrong — and they are — how on earth does that help a new investor? Well, as I suggested above, you listen carefully to what they say but you don't do as they say. If you want to profit, do the opposite of what the experts say.

At the end of 2017, the experts who gave an opinion said the market would advance, by 6.60 percent on average. Instead it declined by 6.24 percent. They not only got it wrong, they guessed the opposite of what the S&P actually did.

We love experts and gurus. They are identical to TV preachers and politicians. Whatever you want to hear, they will tell you. But they always get it dead wrong. No one would even dream of voting for a politician who told the truth. We can't handle the truth. We want our fantasies fulfilled. It won't ever get us to heaven if we watch and listen to the TV preachers but we will feel better about it.

So if the experts predicted the precise opposite of what happened with the S&P in 2018, what does 2019 have in store for us? Take a look at Figure 6.

The experts now believe the S&P will advance by an incredible 23.66 percent in 2019. It might be a good time to be pricing some long-term puts on the S&P. Few stock markets ever go up that much in a year. Any year.

WALL STREET YEAR-END 2019 TARGETS FOR S&P 500

Strategist	Firm	S&P 500 Target	% Above 2018 Close
Dubravko Lakco-Bujas	JP Morgan	3100	23.66%
David Kostin	Goldman Sachs	3000	19.67%
Savita Subramanian	BofA Merrill Lynch	2900	15.68%
Tony Dwyer	Canaccord	3200	27.65%
Tobia Levkovich	Citi	3100	23.66%
Dennis DeBusschere	Evercore ISI	2900	15.68%
Brian Belski	BMO Capital Markets	3150	25.66%
Binky Chada	Deutsche Bank	3250	29.64%
Keith Parker	UBS	3200	27.65%
Barclay's Bank	Maneesh Deshpande	3000	19.67%
Barry Banister	Stifel Nichlaus	2750	9.70%
as of 12/31/18	Median Target	3100	23.66%

Figure 6. Wall Street's year-end 2019 targets for the S&P 500.

Chapter 6
Why Resource Stocks? Why Now?

IF THE WORLD is going to hell in a hand basket — and it is — and the gurus are all full of crap — and they are — and the banks are about to close, why would anyone in their right mind want to invest in resource stocks?

Simple.

Dr. Marc Faber says it best, in every resource conference where he speaks. He goes through the same sequence as I have here; doom and gloom, everything is going to hell. He tells his audience what they should invest in, with that broad Swiss accent. "Everyvon shuud buy a million-dahler Tee Bill."

That wakes up the sleepy punters at the show. All of a sudden everyone is hanging on his every word.

He continues, "You shuud frame it and putt it on zee vorl. Vehn your grandkiddies come over you shuud point to it and say, 'Zat used to be money.'"

He makes a very valid point. When we go into the mother of all depressions during The Great Reset, the pumped-up assets from the last ten years are going to take a giant dump.

If the world is sitting on $250 trillion in debt that we know cannot be paid, those paper assets, including T-Bills, aren't going to be worth very much. Which would you trust more: a piece of paper representing debt which mathematically can never be paid, or shares in a company investing in resources, either in exploration or mining?

The question may sound simplistic, and it is, but it is also a very valid question. Would you rather have a gallon bucket of Monopoly money or a Krugerrand?

I'm going to go into a short discussion about many of the alternatives in resource shares as well as ETFs and physicals, but first I should talk about the different types of gold and silver mining and exploration companies.

Gold and silver resource companies come in three flavors: the majors, the mid-tiers, and the juniors. The juniors are like lottery tickets. They aren't in production yet but are looking for that big find that will jump their stock up 10,000 percent. Perhaps one in a thousand actually accomplishes that. But the natural behavior of the juniors leaves a lot of room for profit, even among those who never make a giant discovery. A saying in the industry is that when the wind is strong enough, even the turkeys fly.

I like the juniors for one important reason: junior resource stocks move 100–300 percent a year, every year. They did so in 2018, and 2018 was a very boring year without much movement. In 2016 the junior lottery tickets were moving 200–800 percent. Those who are unfamiliar with the junior resource sector should give it a gander by considering something they may not know. If you were to learn how to tell if you are in a bear or a bull market, and how to know when to invest and (even more important) how to sell, you could make a lot of money.

I track about 30 stocks and often own more. Below I show some typical yearly moves I have taken off Stockwatch today from my own account. And do take note, 2018 didn't do much of anything, up or down.

yearly low ($)	yearly high ($)
0.0753	0.181
0.78	1.94
0.035	0.105
1.89	6.42
0.085	0.19
0.025	0.11
0.19	0.50
0.025	0.11
0.085	0.19
0.21	0.69
0.30	1.96
0.01	0.80
0.0719	0.2048
0.09	0.26
0.025	0.115
0.17	0.52
0.085	3.60
0.14	0.35
0.07	1.90
0.13	0.59
0.075	0.65
0.055	0.15
0.05	0.09
0.06	0.11
0.055	0.18

If you look at that table closely, you will realize that it is rare for a company to move less than 100 percent in a year, between low and high. And some moves, such as buying shares at seven cents and selling at $1.90, are a once-in-a-lifetime opportunity to profit.

By the way, you will never ever do that; nobody catches both the top and the bottom. But if you are investing to make a profit, and a few people actually are, if you caught half the gain from the low to the high in a year, you would have a nice double-digit percentage profit. Every year.

I've done very well by doing nothing more than putting in stink bids below the yearly low and asks above the yearly high. If nothing else has changed and I like a stock at a given price I am always happy to buy more at a lower price. Likewise, I invest to make money, and if a stock moves higher than it's been in the last year, I am often fine with selling some shares into a new yearly high.

There is one thing I should include here: the basic liquidity of the market is an indication of where you are. At market bottoms you can't give shares away; at tops, the market has total liquidity. So if you can sell shares easily, that is often a great indication of when to sell.

People tend to make investing in juniors way too complicated. It shouldn't be complicated and it's easy to learn how to profit.

I'm going to show you how to do it, but you have to discard almost all of what you think you know. You have to learn the basics of investing that no one has ever bothered teaching you. You know how to add. You know how to read. You probably have some special skill that someone is willing to pay you for doing well. But as far as I know, there are no classes on how to invest, and if you are to profit, you have to know the basics.

Nearly all investors lose money. If you are in that large group, once you read this book you will realize that it is a voluntary position to be in. That's right, most people lose money. You have to unlearn the bad habits. Most people can't or won't do it.

If you aren't willing to learn a new way of thinking and acting, you might as well stop reading the book right here, as it will be a waste of your time to continue. I'm perfectly fine with you staying in the group that always loses money.

If there were not a lot of people in that group, how on earth do you think I would be able to make money? I don't make any money because I am so smart; I get all my profit because other people are so foolish.

Chapter 7
The Secret No One Wants You to Know

A WHILE AGO I WROTE A PIECE that I called *Sentiment indicates extremes of emotion for lots of commodities*. It was posted on January 25, 2018 on StreetwiseReports.com (the Appendix gives details). In it, I talked about the Daily Sentiment Index, or DSI.

I have a subscription to the DSI service (again, see the Appendix). I had noticed that the sentiment indicators for a whole bunch of commodities were showing extreme readings.

In the article I predicted that an even dozen commodities would change direction. If they had been going up, they would turn down. If they had been going down, they would turn up. All 12 did. I have never heard of anyone predicting turns on a dozen commodities and getting it right.

The top for the S&P turned out to be on January 26, one day after my story appeared. My writing wasn't based on voodoo or magic. It wasn't because I am some sort of expert. Every word I wrote was based on facts and numbers I got from a service that anyone can access.

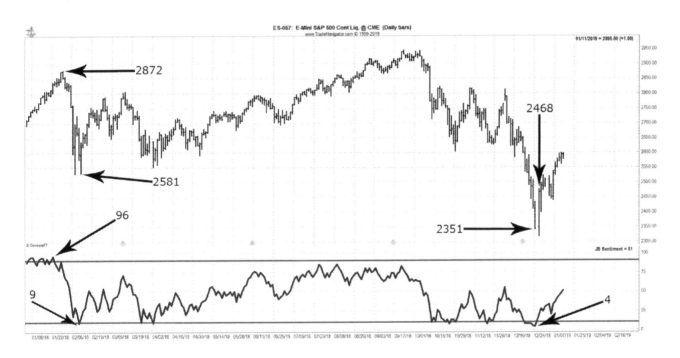

Figure 7. The S&P 500 and the DSI in 2018.

Figure 7 above shows both a turn at the high in January of 2018 and a crash and recovery in December of 2018. A Daily Sentiment Indicator showing an extreme of emotion such as above 95 or below 5 doesn't necessarily tell you the timing of the crash; it just says it is on the way. After bouncing along above 90 for a couple of weeks, the high point for the DSI was at 96 on January 22. The market crashed only four days later. A measure of 96 is extreme. Any extreme of that magnitude, in either direction, says: big crash or big climb, soon.

The DSI is a gauge of sentiment. It ranges from one to 100. If a commodity has a reading of one, it means everyone hates it. A reading of 100 means that everyone loves it.

As the DSI numbers become more extreme in either direction they become more important and more valid. It's possible to get a turn in direction with a reading of 10 or 90, but readings of 3 or 97 say it's turning now, right now. Silver got to 97 in April of 2011, at the very top. Even at the very highest price silver ever reached, in January of 1980 at $50.25 an ounce, it was at only 94.

Just to see if I still had the touch, I posted another article on sentiment on December 24, 2018: *Sentiment Says, Turn, Turn, Turn* (see the Appendix). This time I remarked that 11 of the 40 commodities tracked by the DSI were at or near extremes of emotion. I believed they would turn. The DSI for the S&P was down at 4 that day, and the reading for the VIX touched 97.

It was not only those 11 commodities that turned. The Dow made a record climb the day after plunging on December 24. The VIX reversed and dropped by 10 percent in one day. Those are giant moves. And you can predict the same things yourself. You have access to the same data I have. It isn't magic.

In early December of 2018, after the market had been plunging since September, the DSI started bouncing along below 10, telling those watching that a turn was near. I saw the low of 4 on December 24 and said there would be a major turn. And it happened just that way. You can do the same.

Imagine for a moment that you are in a room — a very big room, mind you — that contains representatives of every investor in the world. If every single one of them agrees that basketballs are going to go up in price, the DSI for basketballs would have a reading of 100. So if the DSI for basketballs is 100, what do you suppose will happen on the very next trade?

Exactly right.

When everyone agrees price will go up, the only thing that can happen is that price will go down because there are no more buyers left, only sellers. Likewise, when everyone agrees the price of basketballs is going down, you will have run out of sellers and price has to go up.

It's called contrarian investing, and it is part of the secret that the gurus don't want you to either understand or know about, and certainly not to use. If you understand the key to profitable investing in different markets, you would never need to know anything more about the commodity than what people think about its price. Now I have already shown you that the experts are always wrong. Sentiment measures not only the gurus but shows what all investors feel about any particular investment.

The mob is always wrong. All you have to do is figure out what they think and then do the opposite. There are a variety of different measures of sentiment. The DSI is only one.

It stands to reason that if people are thinking about making an investment in something, gold for example, they might go to Google and type in, "Gold as an investment." We can go to Google Trends and track just how many people have used that phrase during the last 14 years.

As it turns out, the searches on Google for "gold as an investment" peaked in August of 2011, just before gold peaked at $1,921 an ounce in early September. Google allows you to look back to 2004 so we know that the very highest reading for that phrase was just before the peak price for gold.

Figure 8 shows the results on Google Trends over the period 2014–18.

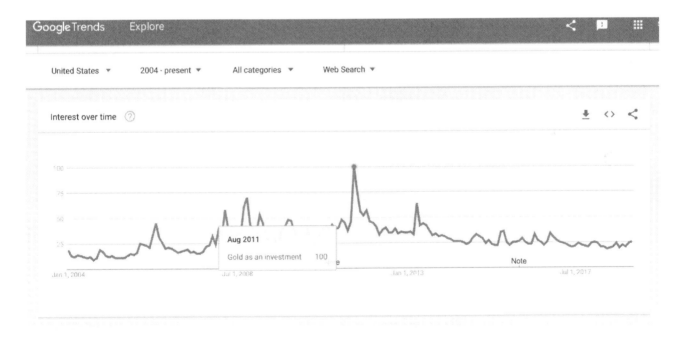

Figure 8. Google Trends: Gold as an investment, 2004–18.

But different commodities have different cycles. What do you suppose you would get if you went again to Google and typed in "Silver as an investment"?

Figure 9. Google Trends: Silver as an investment, 2004–18.

Well, take a look at Figure 9 above. Bear in mind that silver peaked at just under $50 an ounce in late April of 2011, having risen from a low of $4.01 in late November of 2001. We had an earlier peak in 2005, from which the price of silver had tumbled once before. Here, Google Trends shows interest in silver also peaking in April of 2011, right at the high.

One of the all-time classic pieces I wrote was posted on 321gold.com, my metals site, on April 25, 2011. I called the piece *Facts on Silver.* (See the Appendix for details.) I used data from the Sprott Physical Silver Trust (PSLV) website.

Figure 10 on the next page is taken from the Sprott website. It shows the premium for this silver ETF peaking on April 19, 2011. On that day, the premium was more than 25 percent. In other words, if silver had been priced at $40 on that day, investors were willing to fork over $50 an ounce for the silver ETF, a 25 percent premium. Now that's plain daft, but people overshoot on investments all the time.

Facts on Silver won me the most hate mail of any article I had ever written, until I predicted the peak of Bitcon in December of 2017. If you are really willing to become a true contrarian, you will find out that the number of people who tell you that they hate you will be very high. People don't like having their bubbles burst, and they will blame you for it, even if all you do is point out that it is a bursting bubble.

{38}

Figure 10. Sprott PSLV: premium vs. NAV, 2011.

As an investor, you must use every possible sentiment indicator you can get your hands on. As it turns out, the Daily Sentiment Indicator had been flashing warning signs for two months before the 2011 top.

As shown in Figure 11 on the next page, the DSI first touched 96 on February 23, 2011 and bounced along for the next two months. On April 19 the premium on the PSLV ETF hit 25 percent and I knew the crazies had taken over the nuthouse. I looked for a spike in silver, and it popped on April 25, marking the major top for silver for at least the next eight years.

If investors were willing to pay a 25 percent premium to buy into a silver ETF at the top of the market in 2011, what do you suppose is happening with the same commodity on the same website today? Now this gets interesting because it suggests that silver is due a big rally now, based on an almost total absence of interest in silver.

I am trying to get readers to understand that sentiment is the most important key to successful investing, and that there are a variety of ways to measure sentiment.

Figure 11. Silver and the DSI in 2011.

Figure 12. Sprott PSLV: discount vs. NAV, 2018–19.

Figure 12 shows the same Sprott PSLV chart as Figure 10, but this time for 2018–19 instead of 2011. It shows that on November 5, 2018 you could buy silver at a 5.37 percent discount through Sprott. The yearly low price for silver for 2018 was on November 14. Savvy investors had a week's warning from the Sprott PSLV silver ETF.

In Figure 12, I think the big spike in the discount to silver after the November 5 low is actually nothing more than bad data. That happens, too.

We have a variety of sentiment indicators available to us. Wise investors will use all that they can access. Naturally, the PSLV premium and discount chart is free, but no less valuable for that. The DSI from Jake Bernstein costs money but one good trade can more than pay for the service. The DSI for silver for 2018 showed a reading of just 9 on November 9, 12, and 13. Combined with the warning of a low provided by the PSLV chart, putting the two indicators together makes for a clear picture.

In 2011 gold did about the same thing as silver. On July 13, nearly two months before the final all-time high for gold, the DSI touched 94; see Figure 13 below. It bounced along slightly above and slightly below 90 for the next two months before hitting an amazing extreme of emotion in August. On August 19 and 22 the DSI touched 98, for a record high as measured on the DSI. Gold peaked on August 22 and retested the high at $1,921 two weeks later.

Figure 13. Gold and the DSI in 2011–12.

On my own site we track the number of visitors we get daily. It gives me a free glimpse of what potential investors are thinking. In 2011, at the height of the gold and silver markets, we got as many as 125,000 visitors a day. With gold and silver being unpopular today, we are down to 35,000 to 40,000 visitors coming to us daily. Nothing about the website has changed other than the number of people wanting to know about gold, silver, and resource companies. It's the same site, but with 30 percent of the interest seen eight years ago. That makes for a good measure of sentiment as well.

Investment advice and information comes in two flavors, signal and noise. That which is signal gives you potentially valuable information that you can use to make intelligent investment decisions. But noise does little more than confuse the listener.

Not everything you hear or read helps you. The Internet has just made it worse. Every nutcase in the world now has an agenda and a website. You can read about everything from aliens to new scams for you to invest in.

Among the greatest contrarian indicators I knew of were stories above the fold in the *Wall Street Journal* and the *New York Times*, or on the covers of *Fortune* or *Forbes* magazine. By the time the writers for those institutions had figured out there was a new investment to look at, it would have become the last big thing. Showing up on the cover of *Forbes* was like the kiss of death.

I miss those indicators but there is a far bigger group of sentiment indicators available for those who understand them.

I do want to warn potential investors in anything that the basic level of both knowledge and predictive ability of most newsletter writers and website operators is abysmal. My estimate is that 90 percent of what I read and see is pure hogwash that the writer has made up to sell subscriptions.

It's a truism of newsletter writers, politicians and TV preachers that they suck up money and votes from the public by telling people what they want to hear. I know of dozens of writers who simply make shit up. I go into this at some length in *Nobody Knows Anything* and made myself very popular among the swamp we call "analysts" and who try to define themselves as experts.

Maybe ten percent are worth reading at all. There must be 40 or 50 websites calling themselves junior resource sites. I visit three or four and no more. The rest are timewasters, doing little more than parroting what some other fool had to say about something he knew nothing about.

That is not to say there are no people or sites providing valuable data. There are some wonderful thinkers and writers. I have added a list in Chapter 14 of some of the very best, for you to consider. I love listening to John Rubino and reading Bob Hoye and Grant Williams. They make you think and question what you believe.

What I have found is that it tends to be more valuable (as an investment aid) to disagree with what you are being told. If all you read is what you agree with, that is confirmation bias. You read it because you believe it. But reading what you don't necessarily agree with will teach you far more, because it requires you think about what you believe, and why. If you don't change your opinion when provided with better information, you are stuck in a rut and will never make money.

Chapter 8
Why 85%–95% of Investors Lose Money

LIKE SCHOOLS OF FISH, flocks of birds and herds of sheep, humans have a need to be part of the group. We do things because that's what everyone around us is doing. In nature, being part of the band can protect you from predators. Most certainly the financial arena is filled with voracious predators.

In finance it is nothing but a guaranteed way to lose money. Follow the herd, lose money. The odds are stacked against you before you even start. Take for example a commodity with a bid of 3.5 and an ask of 4.0. You buy at the bid and sell at the ask. If you make one transaction, buying and then selling, you have lost .5. That's called slippage and it is why most people have to lose. Then you have to add in commissions.

It has to do with the nature of how things are bought and sold. Investors tend to think that the odds of winning and losing are 50–50, but they are not. More than half of all investors have to lose. No matter how good you are at picking investments, you have to overcome the slippage and the commissions before you can make a single penny.

But it gets worse. Nobody wants to buy stocks or commodities when they are going down. They want to wait until they go up. And the higher they go, the more excited investors become, until whatever the investment is goes into a bubble that then bursts.

This is not merely irrational; it goes right into stupid. We don't buy milk or bread because the price just went up. We go to car dealerships to buy a car when they are holding a sale, not because they just doubled the price of the vehicle we want.

When I have done my research into a company, and sentiment indicates low interest in that stock, and I buy some, and the price of the stock then goes down, I buy more. Now that's based on price, not on any fundamental changes in the company. You are only going to make money by buying when things are cheap and selling when they get expensive.

Here we need to touch on when to sell. I have an entire chapter about selling in *Nobody Knows Anything* because it is so important. Many readers have commented that that chapter justifies the price of the entire book. But it's only a ten spot for the book so I'm not sure if I was being complimented or not.

You have been conditioned to be part of the herd. We all are. You have to break that conditioning if you are to make money in investing. The herd always loses, and one big reason why is how and when they sell.

By and large, only two things can happen when you make an investment, no matter what it is. You either profit or you lose. So if you buy a stock that is hot and it goes up by a factor of ten, what do you think most investors will do?

I'll tell you what they *don't* do. I know because I have been as guilty of this as anyone else. I have a great competitive advantage in buying junior resource stocks because many times I have met management and visited the project; I have made 400 or 500 site visits over the last two decades.

Almost every stock I buy has gone up. Then I watch as they fade away because management was blowing smoke up my ass about their plans.

All investments go up and all investments go down. If you refuse to sell when you have a profit, the only alternative is to sell at a loss.

I know someone personally who bought into one of the hottest stocks, early in the 2000–08 bull market in gold. In fact he was a founding investor in the company, at $.30 a share. The company went to almost $20 a share. He didn't sell any shares.

Here is a fact of life. If you buy a great stock and it goes up, the only time you actually make money is when you sell. You have to both buy and sell any investment in order to profit. It's a piece of paper until you close the trade, no matter how many zeroes you think it is worth.

I'll repeat, things go up and things go down. The investor I am talking about rode the shares all the way back down to $.46 in 2008. He made a lifestyle-changing investment and did nothing with it when he could.

In *Nobody Knows Anything* I also tell the story of a farmer from Kansas, and I think they are all farmers in Kansas, who chased me down and called me about a stock he bought after I wrote about it. He bought at $.12 a share and the stock was selling at $.75. He wanted to know what to do. What followed is a good example of common but expensive human behavior so I am going to repeat it here.

I'm not an investment advisor and I can't go telling people what they should do with their money, else the TSX and SEC get very upset. But I can say what I would do in the same situation.

I asked him the most important question I could think of: "Why did you buy this stock?"

He was hesitant but he responded, "Because I want to make money."

That was a nice answer. There are at least a thousand good reasons to sell an investment. Your kids are entering Harvard and you get to pay. You need a new pickup truck. The roof needs fixing. Wifey wants to be taken on a long vacation. Those are all perfectly valid reasons to sell. You should also include, "Because I can sell at a profit."

There is only one valid reason to buy any investment. Because you want to profit.

So I tell the farmer, and he seems like a really nice person, something along the lines of, "If I had a stock that went up over 500 percent I would sell all or part of it. If I sold half, I would not only have more than my initial investment back, I could still go along for the ride in case it wants to go up more. Or I could sell it all and take wifey out to dinner at a really nice restaurant in Honolulu."

I felt pretty good about myself after the call. I had played a small part in putting money into a guy's pocket at no cost to me. He was even kind enough to call me and thank me.

Years went by far quicker than I am comfortable with. I got another phone call from a farmer in Kansas. Given that it's a pretty big state and everyone there is a farmer anyway, what were the chances of it being my farmer from years before?

In any case, farmer 2 and I chatted for a bit and something seemed to click. On a hunch, I asked him, "Didn't you call me once before, asking about that stock XYZ?"

There was a long pause. You might even call it a long, pregnant pause before he spoke. "Well, yes I did."

The long pregnant pause concerned me a lot. People don't usually hesitate for five minutes when you ask a simple, direct question.

I zoomed in. "As I recall, you called me when XYZ was seventy-five cents and asked what you should do. I remember the stock peaked at seventy-six and you had bought at twelve cents. What did you do in the end about the stock?"

There was another long pregnant pause and then a hesitant answer. "Well," he began, "I ended up selling it."

Oftentimes people say more with pregnant pauses and silence at the wrong time than they do when they are speaking.

So I asked another simple and direct question. "What price did you sell it at?"

He sort of mumbled, "Five cents."

He bought the stock at $.12, rode it to $.76 after calling someone and asking for free advice about to what to do at $.75, and then sat on it all the way down to $.05, which happened to be the low. He unloaded it there because it was such a rotten investment. Now that's called snatching defeat from the very jaws of victory.

And that's what 85–95 percent of people do. That's why they lose money. I have done it and no doubt I will do it again in the future. But sink your teeth into this.

Two things can happen when you make an investment. You can make a profit or you can lose money. If you refuse to take a profit, the only other thing that can happen is that you make a loss.

Learn how to buy. Sentiment is a secret ingredient that few writers will ever bother talking about because it's too simple. But in order to profit you must learn how to sell. Make a plan when you buy. When a stock can go up 25 percent in a day

— and in a bull market that happens all the time — why not take it? If you have bought into a company that just made a giant discovery and the stock has tripled, why not sell a quarter or a half of your shares?

Have a plan. Then execute the plan. Make money. Remember this: the only alternative to making money is losing money. If you don't sell at a profit you pretty much guarantee you are going to panic and sell at the bottom. It's the nature of people in groups. Everyone else does it too.

I was buying silver and gold throughout the 1970s. Not a lot; a few hundred dollars at a time, when I could afford it. By January of 1980 I began to get real nervous. All the people I had been trying to convince of the logic of buying the metals were jumping into gold and silver after they had gone up by hundreds of percent.

There was a coin store I used near where I used to live. By mid-January of 1980 there were dozens of people lined up there waiting to buy, and a far shorter line of people waiting to sell.

The fellow running the store paid me a premium for all the silver bars I had. I sold out way too early; it must have been a full week before the top on January 21. I sold all my silver at $35 an ounce. I felt bad because it hit $50 a week later, but I considered myself smart because I had been buying at under $5 an ounce.

I stayed out of the metals until around 2000, when it seemed to me that they were getting pretty cheap. In 2000 and 2001 I was buying 100-ounce silver bars as low as $4 or so an ounce. My dealer had stacks of them. He commented to me that he had been dealing with the same people for 20 years. He remembered selling the bars to people in 1980 and buying the exact same bars back, at a lower price, in 2000.

If you are one of the 85 percent of people who want to buy at tops and sell at bottoms, you are going to be buying from and selling to the 15 percent of people who understand the basics of investing. It's not easy but it is simple. Change your mindset.

No one has ever heard of sheep making money in any investment market. They run around in herds, acting like they are afraid of their own shadows. First they get shorn, then they get slaughtered, then they get eaten. Do you really want to be part of the herd?

Chapter 9
Let Them Eat Cake

WE DON'T YET KNOW how and when the collapse comes. It's coming, we know that, but so is Christmas. But a worldwide revolution would certainly make a good start to the final days of the financial mess central banks and governments have caused.

It was the best of times, it was the worst of times, it was the age of wisdom, it was the age of foolishness, it was the epoch of belief, it was the epoch of incredulity, it was the season of Light, it was the season of Darkness, it was the spring of hope, it was the winter of despair, we had everything before us, we had nothing before us, we were all going direct to Heaven, we were all going direct the other way – in short, the period was so far like the present period, that some of its noisiest authorities insisted on its being received, for good or for evil, in the superlative degree of comparison only.

Those memorable words, penned by Charles Dickens in 1859, begin the story of the times leading up to the French Revolution and ending in the Jacobin Reign of Terror. *A Tale of Two Cities* may return for an encore. So might the Reign of Terror.

The earth's very first worldwide revolution began in Paris on November 17, 2018. The immediate cause was an increase in taxes on diesel and gasoline. In 2018 the French government had levied higher taxes on diesel (an extra 7.6 cents per liter), with a planned increase of an additional 6.5 cents on January 1, 2019. Gasoline taxes rose by 3.9 cents in 2018 and were due to go up another 2.9 cents with the turn of the New Year.

Globalization has caused a mass migration all over the world from rural areas and small towns to the large cities. As the migration took place, the balance of political power shifted and rural areas had less and less influence on the decision-making process.

French law requires that all vehicles be equipped with neon yellow safety vests, in case the automobile is disabled or the driver needs to change a tire. Yellow vests, or *gilets jaunes*, are stored in every car in case of emergency. Any emergency will do, even a revolution.

The protests began simply with a demand that the increases in fuel taxes be rescinded. From Paris, other groups of Gilets Jaunes, as the protesters were soon named, sprang up spontaneously all over France, in village squares and in the ubiquitous traffic circles controlling the flow of traffic rather than the red lights found in most countries. People in the streets protesting actions of the government are the ultimate form of direct democracy.

There were no leaders. At times some labor unions and politicians have attempted to co-opt the movement, without success. The Yellow Vests reject centralized power, no matter where it comes from. All the protests came directly from local residents angry at their voices going unheard.

By and large it was peaceful from the beginning, with the exceptions being mostly on the part of the police. Participants in most cities simply walked around talking to other Yellow Vests. As time went by the list of demands grew to include the resignation of President Emmanuel Macron as well as other changes in forms of taxation and benefit modifications.

Naturally, the elite in government smiled as the requests for change grew out of control. They knew that as the demands expanded, the chance of them being enacted declined.

Under pressure, Macron agreed to postpone or cancel the fuel tax increase and went along with some minor modifications to minimum wage and retirement benefits. But he soon tired of these sops to the masses and began to harden his position.

The Yellow Vest movement is simple. The people want more say in how the government affects their lives.

Politicians are loath to let a good crisis go to waste, so Prime Minister Edouard Philippe announced support for a new law banning unapproved protests.

The idea was not complicated. It's OK to riot but you need to fill out forms in triplicate and get government approval first. I have some advice for the Gilets Jaunes: "Don't hold your breath."

The Yellow Vest masses seemed to touch a nerve with angry people all over the world. It is a worldwide revolution and it will only grow.

For as long as there have been groups gathered together for protection, the elite have ruled. It didn't matter if it was the head of a clan, a Pope, a king, or eventually presidents and prime ministers. The elite ruled and the peasants could stuff themselves with cake if there was no bread. But the elites have always been out of touch with what the people, the mob, peasants, the masses want.

Sometimes, when the peasants had gone hungry for long enough, they manned the barricades and sharpened their pikes. In the end, after every revolution, all they managed to accomplish was to replace one group of elites with a different group of clueless elites. Look at the elections in the US and the UK. One party rules, then the other party rules, then it goes back again. Nothing ever changes.

Who do the Yellow Vests think will take over if they boot Macron? I can tell you right now that it will be another brain-dead idiot determined to line his own pockets at the expense of the public until he too gets the boot.

This process of rule by elites has led to the bizarre situation in the US where a tiny group of determined neocons managed to subvert the entire political and military establishment of the country on behalf of a meaningless little shit-for-brains country in the Middle East. Numbering no more than 30, they still took total control of the establishment and involved the nation in one meaningless and expensive war after another. It has gotten so stupid and out of control that the very first law considered by the US Congress and US Senate was a bill to make boycotts of Israel illegal.

You may still boycott Mormons and Buddhists. It's legal and OK to boycott the Pope or Donald Trump, should you wish. Advocating boycotts of Hillary will still be allowed. You can boycott whoever and whatever you wish. Except for Israel. Twenty-six states have already incorporated rules requiring loyalty oaths to Israel. In Europe you may not question the Holocaust. If you even debate what happened, you may go to jail.

Now that's power.

In an ominous move, the French government just took action that might morph a peaceful protest against petty taxes into a violent reign of terror and a resurrection of the guillotine. And a lot of heads of former elites swinging from long pikes.

It was reported on January 13, 2019 that some units of the riot police had been issued with fully automatic G36 rifles. If and when some fool of a policeman starts shooting at protestors, a bloody war will have started. Eventually more and more of the police will realize they are shooting their own citizens. At that point they will start shooting politicians.

As the Gilets Jaunes protest moved into its third month, the powers that be seemed to be suggesting the government be given even more power to squash the protestors.

A former Minister of Youth for France, Luc Ferry, said, "The police are not given the means to end this violence. It's unbearable. Listen, frankly, when you see guys kick a poor policeman when he's down, that's enough! Let them use their arms once and for all, basta! As I recall, we have the world's fourth army, capable of putting an end to this garbage."

What seems to have lit Ferry's fuse was the suggestion that France pass some sort of Citizens Initiative Referendum; I return to that below. He wrote recently, "The current disparaging of experts and criticism of elitism is the worst calamity of our times."

There is a simple and bloodless solution that the elite will hate and the Gilets Jaunes of all countries will love. But to understand it, you must also understand why these protests have expanded so quickly.

Until the Internet came along 20 years or so ago, the elite ruled because they controlled the narrative. Americans believed that Kennedy was killed by a lone assassin, that the Vietnam war was fought to save the Vietnamese from godless Communism, and that 19 hijackers led by a guy with terminal kidney disease living in a cave in Afghanistan managed to win the most effective battle in history.

Then the Internet gave everyone a voice. Every damned fool given a new keyboard for Christmas by momma could go out on chatboards and say whatever idiotic things they wanted and remain anonymous, and didn't have to account for their stupidity to anyone. If they wished, they could (and did) watch porn from the confines of their jobs in government offices, if that is what they ostensibly did for a living. Communication was instant and total.

A few people posting on the Internet actually made some sense. The Internet is not necessarily a Mecca of accurate information. But some of the voices made sense, and if you ignored the clutter and listened to the bells that pealed with the ring of truth, you would find examples of false flag operations that would have passed with flying colors 50 years ago being exposed in minutes.

More and more of the middle class realized that the actions of governments and central banks were destroying their financial security. There was nothing new about that; governments have always waged war first on their own people. Throughout history, people have resented their standard of living being destroyed by the elite.

But they couldn't do a damned thing about it. They might be angry but they had no voice.

Eventually they could take a marvelous weapon right at hand, such as the Yellow Vests, and make them a symbol of protest. But they still didn't have a solution that was both reasonable and possible until a genius named Etienne Chouard came up with a magic bullet.

Monsieur Chouard teaches college in Marseilles, on the Mediterranean coast of France. For years he has advocated the adoption of something he calls the Citizens Initiative Referendum, or CIR. The CIR asks only that citizens be allowed to choose the rules and regulations by which they are governed, and proposes that the best way to achieve such direct democracy is by way of the referendum.

The concept is brilliant. A certain number of signatories on a petition would allow for a referendum to be published and voted on.

I mentioned in Chapter 2 that the Swiss did it in 2016 with the idea of a guaranteed basic income for all. It was suggested that all Swiss citizens be granted an automatic 2,500 Swiss francs monthly. Naturally, the Swiss, being the Swiss, understood that someone would have to pay for that largesse, and that it would be themselves.

Governments don't have any money; all they do is take it from one group and hand it to another. In the referendum, 77 percent of the Swiss who voted soundly rejected the idea.

A worldwide revolution has been started. It's pretty much led by the middle-class who believe government policies are destroying them financially. If and when the police start shooting at protestors, protestors will start shooting back. It has all the potential for being the greatest war in history. The governments will eventually lose as the police and military change sides.

A well thought-out CIR would solve the issue. It is both practical and workable. The elites will hate it because they will lose their franchise on power and money. The people will love it because it makes them responsible for their own decisions. They should be allowed direct democracy because they are the ones paying for it.

In the end the world will owe a giant debt to Etienne Chouard for his ideas. It may not be a perfect solution but it is a solution. The alternatives are far worse.

We are going to have a collapse; the only question is how we recover.

Chapter 10
The Precious Metals Stocks

OVER 1,200 MINING COMPANIES make their home in Canada. That's just on the TSX and TSX Venture stock exchanges. More can be found on the CNQ Exchange. In 2017 the Canadian mining industry derived $44 billion in revenue from mining companies with a combined market cap of $260 billion. Mining accounts for 3.6 percent of the Canadian economy and 32 percent of its exports.

Australia is the giant in mining, with mining being 5.6 percent of its economy and 35 percent of its exports. Australia is the world's largest producer and exporter of coal, the second-largest producer of iron, fourth-biggest nickel miner, fifth in size for copper mining, and second only to China in gold production.

Some of the world's biggest mining companies are Australia-based, including BHP Billiton, the largest mining company in the world, and Rio Tinto, second-largest in the world.

Canada can brag of Barrick, currently the world's biggest gold producer. But Newmont, one of the few US-based mining companies, intends to take over Goldcorp, and if it does so, that will make Newmont the largest in the world.

The vast majority of my readers are Canadian and American, so I will cover the Canadian shares more deeply than either the Australian or London-listed shares. With only a few exceptions, such as Newmont, the United States has run off most mining companies to relocate in more reasonable jurisdictions.

GOLD STOCKS

Royalty Stocks
Franco-Nevada
Osisko Gold Royalties
Royal Gold
Sandstorm Gold
Wheaton Precious Metals

In May of 2018 someone named Reuben Gregg Brewer wrote a great piece about investing in royalty stocks and posted (see the Appendix) it on The Motley Fool website. It gave a great insight into the sector so I have reposted it here.

⌘ ⌘ ⌘

INVESTING IN PRECIOUS METALS is most often associated with directly owning bullion or investing in mining companies, but both strategies have notable drawbacks. Streaming and royalty companies, like **Royal Gold, Inc., Franco-Nevada Corporation, and Wheaton Precious Metals Corp.,** change the equation, effectively avoiding many of those negatives, allowing them to provide more consistent returns to investors over time. Here are some of the key benefits and drawbacks you need to know about the gold streaming niche, including a deeper look at a few of the industry's biggest companies.

What is gold streaming?

The precious metals mining business is pretty simple to under-stand: Find a spot that contains gold or silver, dig it up, and sell it. That's obviously an oversimplification of a very complex, dangerous, and expensive business model, but you get the idea. A streaming and royalty company doesn't do any of that, but instead provides an important part of the process: cash.

Essentially, streaming provides cash up front to miners in exchange for the right to buy gold, silver, or other metals at reduced rates in the future. Miners benefit from having access to an additional source of capital over and above what they can get from banks and capital markets, which at times can be costly sources of capital. Streaming companies, meanwhile, benefit from contractually locking in low costs for gold and silver.

Many companies that operate in the streaming niche also have royalty deals in their portfolio. Royalty deals are similar to streaming deals in that cash is provided up front to miners. In exchange, however, the miner pays a percentage of the sales from a mine to the streaming and royalty company. The up-front payment is usually larger, since the streaming and royalty company isn't expected to buy any of the gold that is produced from the mine. For the most part, the risks and rewards of royalty and streaming deals are fairly similar.

An example of a streaming deal

In 2015, Royal Gold announced that it had inked a streaming deal with Barrick Gold Corporation, one of the largest gold miners in the world, related to Barrick's 60% interest in the Pueblo Viejo mine in the Dominican Republic. Royal Gold provided the miner $610 million in exchange for 7.5% of Barrick's interest in the gold produced at Pueblo Viejo until 990,000 ounces of gold have been delivered, and 3.75% thereafter, plus 75% of Barrick's interest in the silver produced at the mine until 50 million ounces have been delivered, and 37.5% thereafter.

The gold and silver it will receive is notable, of course, but the really important number here is what Royal Gold is paying for that gold and silver: 30% of the spot price up to key production targets, and then 60% thereafter. It doesn't matter what the spot price at the time is, Royal Gold has locked in wide profits.

Benefits to investing in streaming companies

Since streaming and royalty companies are only providing cash to miners, they are best looked at as specialty finance companies. However, for most investors interested in adding precious metals to a diversified portfolio, they are probably the best option. The reasons tie back to the unique streaming model, which includes contractually locked-in wide margins, as the example above illustrates. Benefits to investors include:

Consistent results. Although each streaming and royalty deal is different, the trailing EBITDA margins of streaming companies Royal Gold, Franco-Nevada, and Wheaton Precious Metals have been solidly positive over the past decade. Positive, and wide, EBITDA margins are a sign these companies are running their businesses profitably. The contractually guaranteed low prices these companies pay are the bedrock on which those consistently wide margins are built. Giant miners like Barrick Gold, Newmont Mining, and Goldcorp, for comparison, have each seen their trailing EBITDA margins dip into negative territory at least once, if not more often, during that same time period.

Fast-moving gold prices and the costs of mining, which is a slow and difficult process, combine to make consistency hard to achieve for miners. And it can be difficult for investors to stick around when a miner is struggling to turn a profit. The wide margins at royalty and streaming companies, on the other hand, can provide a reason for shareholders to stick around even if gold prices are falling.

Diversification means less risk. Diversification is another key benefit streaming and royalty companies offer, with even large miners generally only operating a handful of mines. Some small miners, meanwhile, only operate one or two. Streaming companies, however, generally spread their risk across a larger number of assets. Focusing on providing cash to the miners who take on the task of running mines makes diversification easier for them to achieve. Franco-Nevada, for example, provides exposure to nearly 300 mine investments, 50 of which are producing assets, while the rest are in some stage of development. That diversification materially reduces the risk that trouble at any one mine will derail performance. Since gold and silver prices are already prone to swift and often large price swings, with their prices driven by supply and demand (and often emotional investors), diversifying mine risk is a nice benefit.

Dividends. Dividend income is another key benefit provided by the larger gold royalty and streaming companies. Although miners often pay dividends, too, those can wind up being cut when commodity prices fall. Royal Gold and Franco-Nevada, on the other hand, have each increased their dividend for at least a decade. And while Wheaton's dividend is variable, it is linked to the company's performance, so investors know beforehand that the dividend is a moving target — but they know the math involved behind the payout.

Locked-in low prices, wide margins, and diversification are what allow streaming companies to be more generous with dividends. This is no small point, since dividends can provide investors something to watch, instead of stock prices, when gold and silver prices are weak. That, in turn, can help investors stick around through the entire commodity cycle to benefit from the diversification that gold and silver provide to an investment portfolio.

Better than bullion. Investing in streaming companies also has a leg up on direct ownership of gold and silver. If you buy gold bullion, the only upside you have is a potential increase in the price of gold. An ounce of gold today will still be an ounce of gold tomorrow (or even 1,000 years from now). Since streaming companies invest in both developed and developing mines, they benefit, like miners, from the opportunity for increased production over time. That's one reason that it's important to view streaming companies as having a portfolio, managing a collection of streaming investments over time. Indeed, they need to balance investing in current production with investments that can maintain and enhance production in the future as they are developed.

Risks of investing in streaming companies

There are also issues that investors will want to keep in mind when looking at gold royalty and streaming companies. Since streamers are kind of like specialty finance companies, it shouldn't be surprising at all to know that the biggest issues are found on the balance sheet. This is because the basic streaming model is to use short-term debt to fund streaming and royalty deals and then permanently finance that debt by issuing stock or long-term debt.

Dilution. Some streaming and royalty companies, notably Franco-Nevada, have a preference for maintaining a debt-free balance sheet. However, streaming deals can cost hundreds of millions of dollars. That's not the kind of cash that most companies keep around. So, in order to raise the money needed to support streaming deals, streaming companies often issue stock. The risk here is that every new share of stock reduces the ownership stake, and financial benefit, of existing shareholders.

This dilution, as it's called, isn't a problem if the streaming deals work out as expected. But if something were to go wrong, like a new mine not actually getting built, then issuing dilutive shares would be a notable negative.

Leverage. Other streaming and royalty companies, such as Royal Gold, prefer to use debt to permanently fund their deals. The goal is to use the cash flow from the streaming agreements to reduce the debt balance over time. There are two potential risks here. First, if a mine investment doesn't work out as expected, then the projected cash flows won't be there to pay down the debt or support the associated interest expense. But you'll also want to keep an eye on the total debt load a streaming company is carrying, since too much debt could effectively leave it unable to ink new deals until its balance sheet is healthier.

Are streaming companies good investments?

Streaming and royalty companies aren't right for every investor. For example, if you like to dig in and find unique opportunities being mispriced by the market, the more diversified and hands-off approach of a streamer isn't appropriate for you. And buying gold bullion might be more attractive if you believe gold will be a more viable option in the case of a catastrophic market collapse.

However, for most investors, streaming and royalty companies are a great mix of risk and reward. The diversification, consistently wide margins, and regular dividends can make it much easier to maintain exposure to precious metals throughout the entire commodity cycle. And that, in turn, increases the chance that investors will benefit from the diversification that gold and silver can offer.

⌘ ⌘ ⌘

Majors (production of over one million ounces of gold per year)
Agnico Eagle
AngloGold Ashanti
Barrick Gold
Fresnillo
Goldcorp
Gold Fields
Kinross
Newmont Mining
Newcrest Mining
Randgold Resources
Sibanye-Stillwater
Yamana

Mid-tier (production of over 200,000 ounces of gold per year)
Acacia Mining
Alamos Gold
Asanko Gold
B2Gold
Centamin
Centerra Gold
Coeur Mining
Eldorado
Endeavour Mining
Evolution Mining
Golden Star Resources
Guyana Goldfields
Hecla Mining Company
Hochschild Mining
IAMGOLD
Kirkland Lake Gold
Leagold Mining
New Gold
Northern Star Resources
OceanaGold
Pan African Resources
Perseus Mining
Pretium Resources
Saracen Mineral Holdings
SEMAFO
SSR Mining
Teranga Gold
Torex Gold

Small Producers (some production of gold each year)
Alacer Gold
Alio Gold
Anaconda Mining
Atlantic Gold
Argonaut Gold
Beadell Resources
Belo Sun
Cardinal Resources

Continental Gold

Equinox Gold

Falco Resources

Gold Standard Ventures

INV Metals

Lundin Gold

Mandalay Resources

Orla Mining

Orezone Gold

Osisko Mining

Premier Gold

Project Developers (no production)

Roxgold

Rubicon Minerals

Superior Gold

TMAC Resources

Victoria Gold

Wesdome

Every investor has a different set of requirements, such as the amount of money available to invest, income, willingness to accept risk, age, tax bracket, tax regulations, and purpose of investing in the first place. So there is no one-size-fits-all shoe. You need to know what your limits are and what your goals are. I will give you some of the factors.

There are only a few pure silver producers, and even fewer platinum and palladium companies. So by and large I will cover the gold companies. The reader will have to figure out what applies to his or her particular situation and what the options are.

Anyone who does not have some physical precious metals where they can put their hands on them, no matter what stupidity the government comes up with, is swimming naked and the tide is going out. Don't get caught short.

You don't give a hoot if you own five one-ounce Maple Leafs and the price of gold goes down. Physical metals are insurance against chaos of all sorts. Don't even think about storing them in a safety deposit box. Those have been renamed under the truth in advertising laws to unsafe deposit boxes, and are the first place governments and banks will go to steal when the flag goes up.

You wouldn't drive a car or own a house without insurance. How about tossing a few pennies towards saving your financial future?

EXCHANGE-TRADED FUNDS

Shelia Olson wrote a good piece for Investopedia.com (see the Appendix) in October of 2018, explaining the metals ETFs and how they function.

⌘ ⌘ ⌘

THE PRECIOUS METALS MARKET is always a volatile space – and exchange-traded funds (ETFs) can be a good way for investors to gain exposure through a diversified portfolio.

After a rough couple of years, precious metals did fairly well in 2017, with metals producers reporting some of the top gains. In terms of ETFs, the granddaddy of them all – the SPDR Gold Trust – is up over 10% year to date (YTD), which looks pretty good if you're into pure exposure to precious metals. However, there are other precious metals ETFs that look even better.

Money flowed into precious metals ETFs in 2017, with a number of catalysts increasing demand. The sector stands to gain further as traditional investors seek security from what many believe to be the top safe haven investment category in the investment industry. Many investors find it to be a hedge against uncertainty with factors such as interest rate hikes, currency fluctuations in China and India, the relative strength of the U.S. dollar against global currencies and turmoil in major European banks influencing demand.

If you're looking for a way to build exposure to precious metals as a potential safe haven, these ETFs, chosen on the basis of a combination of assets under management and performance, may be a great place to start your search. All figures are as of December 22, 2017. These funds do not include leveraged investing.

The VanEck Vectors Rare Earth/Strategic Metals ETF (REMX)
* *Issuer: VanEck*
* *Assets under management: $152.2 million*
* *YTD performance: 75.56%*
* *Expense ratio: 0.61%*
* *Price: $28.96*

The VanEck Vectors Rare Earth/Strategic Metals ETF has a year-to-date (YTD) return of 75.56% through December 22, 2017. This ETF invests in companies involved in producing and refining strategic metals and minerals. It is an index fund which seeks to track the performance and returns of the MVIS Global Rare Earth/Strategic Metals Index.

32% of the Fund is invested in Australian companies. The Fund has 21 holdings. Top holdings in the Fund include Pilbara Minerals, Lithium Americas, Tronox and Galaxy Resources. The Fund has a three-year annualized total return of 8.86%.

The ETFS Physical Palladium Shares (PALL)
- *Issuer: ETF Securities*
- *Assets under management: $235.9 million*
- *YTD performance: 52.17%*
- *Expense ratio: 0.60%*
- *Price: $99.23*

Palladium is hot right now partly because automakers are increasingly choosing it for catalytic converters over the more costly alternative platinum, a long-term trend that shows no signs of abating any time soon.

PALL tracks the spot price of palladium based on physical holdings of palladium bullion in JPMorgan vaults in Zurich and London. Volumes are decent, so there is no problem with liquidity. As far as holding costs, this fund's expense ratio is a bit high for a precious metals-backed fund, but if you're looking for pure exposure to palladium, this is really the only fund worth a look.

This fund has returned 52.17% in 2017. Three- and five-year annualized total returns are 8.02% and 8.28%, respectively.

The iShares MSCI Global Select Metals & Mining Producers ETF (PICK)
- *Issuer: iShares*
- *Assets under management: $411.19 million*
- *YTD performance: 35.24%*
- *Expense ratio: 0.39%*
- *Price: $33.84*

PICK is another popular ETF investing in stocks of metal and mining producers. It is indexed to the MSCI ACWI Select Metals & Mining Producers Ex Gold & Silver IMI, which excludes major gold and silver mining companies like Goldcorp Inc. and thus includes more integrated mining companies for a more diversified approach.

There are 186 equities in its basket of holdings with 24% of companies in the U.K. Top holdings in the Fund include BHP Billiton, Rio Tinto, and Glencore. In 2017 the Fund had a return of 35.24% through December 22. Over the past three years, the Fund has annualized total return of 7.75%.

The SPDR S&P Metals & Mining ETF (XME)
- *Issuer: State Street SPDR*
- *Assets under management: $869.4 million*
- *YTD performance: 18.43%*
- *Expense ratio: 0.35%*
- *Price: $35.55*

The SPDR S&P Metals & Mining ETF has a YTD return of 18.43%. Over the past three years, it has an annualized total return of 7.44%. XME is an index fund which seeks to track the holdings and performance of the S&P Metals and Mining Select Industry Index. This index includes metals and mining companies from the S&P TMI.

The Fund has 29 holdings. Top holdings in the Fund include Consol Energy, Allegheny Technologies and Alcoa.

The SPDR Gold Trust (GLD)
- *Issuer: State Street SPDR*
- *Assets under management: $33.98 billion*
- *YTD performance: 10.34%*
- *Expense ratio: 0.40%*
- *Price: $120.94*

The SPDR Gold Trust is the industry's largest precious metals ETF by assets. As of December 22, 2017, assets under management were $33.98 billion. This ETF was the industry's first fund to track the price of gold. It is also the first ETF to be backed by the physical asset. Its return seeks to match the performance of gold bullion's price.

In 2017, the fund has a YTD return of 10.34%. Over the past three years, it has an annualized total return of 2.43%.

The Bottom Line
The effectiveness of gold, silver, and platinum at beneficially diversifying an investor's portfolio is abundantly clear. However, obtaining these benefits requires knowing your personal tolerance for risk and investment goals before diving in. There is an inherent volatility in the precious metals market that indeed can be used as a wealth-building tool but without diligence and forethought, this volatility can also spell ruin for a portfolio. Professional monitoring and appropriate risk management practices have to be applied in any case.

⌘ ⌘ ⌘

Gold, silver, platinum and palladium can also be bought via other various ETFs such as the Sprott Physical Bullion Trusts. Sprott now also owns and runs what was the Central Fund of Canada, called the CEF. I like those particular ETFs a lot because each has a chart showing its historical premium or discount to the net asset value (see Figures 10 and 12, back in Chapter 7). That is like having a free $1,000 annual service giving you the sentiment for any of the metals, gold, silver, and platinum/palladium.

For the many investors who don't have the time or patience to watch and trade shares on a daily or weekly basis, gold mutual funds may be a good choice. These are not ETFs; rather, they are funds with a specific objective and that invest in individual companies. They are great in rising or bull markets and suck in declining markets. If the investor is patient and knows when a major bottom has passed, gold and silver mutual funds are an excellent choice. Don't stay at the party once a major top is in. Like everything else, you have to sell in order to profit.

Here is an article from Gold Bullion Pro (see the Appendix) on gold mutual funds.

⌘ ⌘ ⌘

Top 10 Gold Mutual Funds

Essentially, investors in gold markets have three choices when it comes to selecting a specific mechanism, namely, invest in physical bullion, mining stocks or funds that are managed by professionals whose are responsible for conducting all necessary fund transactions and virtually deciding whether the fund should purchase bullion, mining companies' shares or both. Finding the best fund is your key to successful precious metals investing providing diversification, risk management and hedge against inflation.

Let's take a look at top 10 funds who have proven to be successful players on the market.

1. SPDR Gold Shares (GLD)
With a five star rating and excellent history it is no wonder that GLD is listed as one of the best gold ETF choices available for investors.

2. USAA Precious Metals (USAGX)
Trading since 1984 and with no load fees charged, USAGX is based in the USA and makes the top ten list for best gold investment funds.

3. Tocqueville Gold (TGLDX)
With a nine percent turnover and possible gold options and gold futures holdings at times, Tocqueville Gold is one of the top gold mutual funds for investors interested in this sector.

4. Oppenheimer Gold And Special Minerals A (OPGSX)
This is one of the top rated gold mutual funds, and it is a very popular choice for many investors. Capital appreciation is the goal of the fund, and it has a solid history.

5. Van Eck International Investor Gold A (INIVX)
The Van Eck International Investor Gold A is one of the top gold mutual funds according to investors. You should know that there is a front load fee of 5.75 five percent with this fund though.

6. AIM Gold And Precious Metals Investor (FGLDX)
The FGLDX fund views gold as investment potential and has been ranked one of the top mutual funds in this sector.

7. American Century Global Gold Investor (BGEIX)
BGEIX is one of the top gold mutual funds, in part because of the excellent return offered over the last year, which was more than sixty percent.

8. Franklin Gold And Precious Metals A (FKRCX)
FKRCX is one of the gold mutual funds that charges a front load, but many investors feel the one year return of more than seventy four percent is well worth the load fee charged.

9. DWS Gold And Precious Metals A (SGDAX)
This is one of the funds listed as a top ten because of past performance. It has been trading since 2001 and is now managed by Pierre Martin.

10. OCM Gold (OCMGX)
OCMGX has more than one hundred and forty million in assets, and offers a recent return of more than sixty five percent. Even though this fund does not invest in physical bullion it is still a top ten pick for most investors.

⌘ ⌘ ⌘

I will tell you flat out that if you do not make sentiment your primary timing tool for buying and selling the metals as well as mining shares, you are just throwing your money away. But don't panic if you do. I will be standing there with my hat open in front of me, ready to catch your money, because I do use sentiment to tell me what to do and when to do it.

The few major mining companies should be thought of as elephants or giant ships. They don't go very fast and are hard to turn. The majors pretty much trade with the price of gold. You have excellent liquidity but not much leverage. They are safe but boring. The major mining companies would have been called the trade for widows and orphans in the old days. They won't make you rich but neither will they make you poor.

If you want to make money with the big companies, buy and sell them based only on extremes of emotion. Should you listen carefully and pay attention, a low dividend at $1,300 gold becomes a big dividend at $2,000 gold.

The majors find a good home in ordinary brokerage accounts. You shouldn't need to trade them often and they should provide better long-term capital gains than the mid-tier companies and the juniors.

The mid-tier mining companies also offer excellent liquidity, plus higher leverage to the price of gold and silver. All of them receive coverage from brokers and newsletter writers.

Remember that all of those guys want your money, so you don't have to trust them. Ask around and figure out which are the best writers and thinkers. Here too, sentiment should be your major indicator. Mid-tier shares might be suitable for either an ordinary brokerage account or a RRSP or IRA account where you don't get whacked for taxes on trading.

While I am talking about brokerage accounts, first of all, never trust a broker. I suppose by now most investors have switched to discount brokers, but if you are still using the horse and buggy to get to work, remember that all brokers are liars working for their own self-interest and not yours.

I have lost plenty of money listening to brokers go on and on about something that is a near sure thing. They promise they will keep you advised if anything goes wrong, and then they watch silently as the company eases its way into the bankruptcy that they knew was coming all along.

If you are trading Canadian-based stocks, trade the Canadian symbol only. An OTC symbol for a Canadian stock is a derivative. You are not trading the stock, you are trading a derivative, and often the indicated stock quote will be incorrect.

Find a discount broker who will allow you to buy and sell Canadian stocks using the Canadian symbol in Canadian funds. I had an account for years with Penntrade in Coeur d'Alene, Idaho. They are the online trading division of Paulson Investment

LLC and are nice people to work with. I think trades there are $29.99. It works out a bit cheaper than the cheapest of the cheap discount brokers because they do better executions. If you insist on trading the US OTCBB symbol, you are going to get humped for half a cent or more on every share you trade. And they don't kiss you, either.

In a bull market and when the winds are high enough, even the turkeys fly. In a bear market even the very best of stocks go down. Know where you are in the cycle. The vast majority of writers and commentators don't know what phase we are in at any time. We are either in a bull phase or a bear phase. Everything goes up and goes down. You hit one extreme of emotion, then reverse and continue until you hit the other extreme of emotion.

Those few investors who want to join the ranks of the 5%–15% who actually do make money regularly have to be aware of both the risks and the rewards of investing in junior resource stocks. You can lose money faster in the junior market than in any other investment, as stocks often go up ten percent in a day and may then tumble ten percent the next day. You can also make more money than you can in anything else.

You must know the nature of the beast. The junior mining companies are far too numerous to list here. They are constantly being born and living and dying, just in Canada. In Australia they are more common than the flies during summer in Western Australia. They are lottery tickets first and foremost. Even if you somehow become the smartest and best investor in the junior sector, you are still going to lose money on most of the companies you invest in. Nobody gets them all right and if you profit on half of those you pick, you are doing very well.

The shares are similar both to a lottery ticket with an expiration date coming soon and a baseball trading card. You cannot profit by buying and holding them until they hatch. They aren't duck eggs. If you are going to make money consistently, you have to trade them.

I don't have a chart going back that far, but NovaGold would be a great example. Jay Taylor recommended them at $.30 a share Canadian in early 2001. No one listened and the shares dropped to a low of $.13. I took an interest in the company because they were earning $.13 a share for the year selling gravel in Nome, Alaska. Hell, there couldn't be all that much risk for company earning $.13 and selling for $.13.

I had just started 321gold.com in the summer of 2001. In late August that year I interviewed Greg Johnson and wrote the company up. At that point they had five employees. The company president's wife was an employee. The head of exploration lived in Anchorage, Rick Vanalphabet lived in the Bay area, Greg Johnson lived north of Seattle in a yurt, and the accounting was done in Nova Scotia.

Investors were so starved of information about junior resource companies in 2001 that all you had to do was write about a company and the stock price would double. NovaGold doubled after my first piece. They kept releasing results. I wrote about them again six weeks later and they doubled again.

NovaGold eventually went from a low of $.13 to a high near $20 a share a few years later. If you held on and sold at the high you would have made a life-changing investment. The company was the number one gainer in Canada in 2001.

So far, I am certain readers would conclude that NovaGold was a great stock to buy. Alas, from near $20 it went to a low of $.46 in the dismal days of 2008. You will hear me repeat this again and again because it is so important. All investments go up and all investments go down. Nothing goes straight up and nothing goes straight down.

If you are going to play in the junior playground you have to trade your shares. NovaGold was a great long and it was also a great short. Every other junior is going to do exactly the same thing.

This is where learning to sell becomes almost as important as knowing how to invest using sentiment. You have to be willing to take a profit. Have a plan for selling. If a stock you own doubles or triples, you should be looking to sell some shares. I have seen investors ride a stock to the moon, never sell a single share, and end up being forced out by either wifey or the margin clerk, whichever has the louder voice and the bigger stick.

See if you can find a stock among the thousand or so junior resource stocks similar to Novo Resources. I happen to like this company and its management a lot. I have been following the story for over ten years and writing about it for seven. Novo has been a home run for those willing to take a profit.

Figure 14 on the next page is a chart showing the price action from January of 2018 until January of 2019, as I write this book. NVO began 2018 at $3.25 and then dropped by $.75, or over 20 percent. That's one profit opportunity; either to short it at $3.25 or to go long at $2.50. Then it went up by $1 in two weeks, to $3.50. If you had gone long at $2.50 you now had a chance to sell with a 40 profit in two weeks.

The stock then drops again, this time to $3, before shooting higher to $5.75 in seven weeks. You could have almost doubled your money. Annualized, that's about a 500 percent return. If you are not happy with a 500 percent return, why are you investing at all? Then it dropped by $1.25 for another 20 percent potential return before zooming to $6.43 for another potential $2.20 a share return on investment.

If all you did was to track Novo, and you were willing to both buy and sell, you could damn near day-trade the shares for a 1,000 percent return yearly. I don't do it because I am too lazy but when Novo shares got stupid last year, I did lighten up, and I happen to be one of the biggest believers in the story.

Figure 14. Novo Resources 2018–19.

If you find a single stock that has good liquidity and goes both up and down as the Novo chart reflects, you could make a trade or two a month and make a lot of money. The sentiment for gold and silver will tell you the general state of the market, and then just sell when you can.

Do note that liquidity for companies all by itself is an important sentiment indicator. At bottoms you can't give the shares away and at tops everyone wants in at the same time. So put in stink bids under the low, and when you catch yourself starting to believe along with the rest of the herd that it's going to the moon tomorrow, sell.

Do note that in order to be taking 30–40 percent profits regularly, you will need to be buying and selling the appropriate symbol — Canada for Canadian shares, not OTCBB — and you have to keep track of your tax situation and be dealing with a low-cost, efficient brokerage firm.

The junior mining companies offer incredible leverage to the price of gold and silver. When you have a clear indicator of a bottom in the metals, such as the Sprott physical metals ETF showing the highest discount to its net asset value since the fund began trading (I refer you again to Figure 12), you can risk the real penny dreadfuls below $.10 and below $3 million market cap. They may not discover a bonanza grade mine but they might get caught up in the hurricane as the mob rushes to buy into a resource boom.

SILVER STOCKS

Canadian
Alexco
Endeavour Silver Corp
First Majestic Silver Corp
Fortuna Silver Mines
Great Panther Corp
Group 10 Resources
Hecla Mining
Impact Silver
Mag Silver
Maya Gold and Silver
Pan American Silver
Sierra Metals
Silver Bull Resources
Silvercorp Metals
SSR Mining
Silver Wheaton
Tahoe Resources
Wheaton Precious Metals Corp

London Stock Exchange
Fresnillo (Mexico-based, and the world's largest silver producer)

While I am a big fan of trading the gold resource shares, I'm not nearly as big a fan of trading the silver resource stocks. For some reason even the shares with the greatest liquidity, such as Pan American Silver and First Majestic Silver, don't have all that much leverage to the price of silver.

For myself, I am happier to trade the metal itself. I am always happy to own the metal. You have 100 percent liquidity with tiny commissions due to the tightness between the bid and the ask.

Silver investors are pretty loopy. The information on the Internet about the manipulation of silver and price suppression and how "silver's going to $100 an ounce" is easily the biggest bunch of nonsense I have ever read.

With the exception of David Morgan, who I respect, the guys who write about silver are crazy as shithouse rats. No commodity has ever cost the bulls as much money as silver has, because of the absence of ethics among those commenting on the metal.

Silver is a precious metal. Like gold, it can serve as an insurance policy against government stupidity and financial chaos. But it's not running out. There is no shortage, there never has been a shortage and never will be a shortage. Comex cannot default.

Because this small group of writers utterly lacking in honesty specialize in telling readers just what they want to hear, silver investors get killed on a regular basis.

Up until the crash of everything in October of 2008, a fellow named Jason Hommel was pimping silver to beat the band. He and I were on a panel together in Chicago in late March of 2008. I said I thought silver was going to go down as the market was entering what I predicted would be a major crash. Hommel "guaranteed" it would go up. It crashed from $21 an ounce, where he had been buying, to under $9 an ounce when the crash I had predicted took place. He blew himself up financially because he was unable to understand that all commodities go up and down.

Silver goes down both further and faster than any other commodity I know of. If you can time it with sentiment, going short silver is one of the greatest investment moves you will ever make. Silver is an investment and an insurance policy. It is not a religion.

In 2011, as silver neared $50 an ounce, a guy named Chris Duane popped out of nowhere claiming to be a silver expert and literally demanded I post a piece he had written touting silver as the greatest investment ever. At $35 and $40 and $45 silver, he was telling people to sell everything they had to buy silver, and even to borrow the money. He went so far as to sell his house to buy silver, he was so convinced it would continue to go up.

I told him that I would post a piece by him if he wrote something about how dangerous it was to own silver at a top, because it tended to crash suddenly rather than just decline. He was convinced that I was a fool. I knew he was.

Silver crashed after I called the top to the day. I got tons of nasty e-mails telling me how stupid I was. He blew up financially and lost everything. He cost all the sheep following him hundreds of millions of dollars. He loved silver at $45 an ounce. I wonder how he liked it at under $14 in early 2016, only five years later.

There will be a Chris Duane or a Jason Hommel or a Ted Butler screaming, "Buy" at every top in silver. If you do, you will lose everything.

If you have read my other book on investing, *Nobody Knows Anything*, you will know that in April of 2011 at the top in silver you could have entered a commodity futures trade where you sold silver and bought gold in equal dollar amounts. You could trade the extreme of emotion in silver — more extreme even than in January of 1980, which was the first time silver hit $50 an ounce — by selling what was expensive (silver) and buying what was cheap (gold).

That trade would have been consistently profitable every day from April 25, 2011 until today. You would have made a ton of money and not had to speculate on the direction of the metals.

A similar trade is available today, in reverse. Do you recall me saying that markets move from one extreme to the opposite extreme? As it takes 84 ounces of silver to buy one ounce of gold today, gold is expensive and silver cheap. You could make a lot of money and not have to guess in which directions gold and silver were going to move. Simply sell a dollar amount of gold and buy the same dollar amount of silver. The trade would have been profitable 99 percent of the time over the last 100 years.

Don't make investing complex or listen to those who insist on making it confusing. I have no idea where gold will be tomorrow — or silver, or anything else. But I can say that over the last century you could have traded the gold/silver spread regularly and profited a lot. You don't really need to know where the metals are going if you can figure out what is cheap and what is expensive.

If you recall, I suggested you buy and sell on sentiment, and showed you that there are a variety of sentiment indicators if you only look for them. Stocks going up or down several days in a row is a short-term but still important measure of sentiment.

Stocks go up, stocks go down. In theory, the odds of stocks going up or down is 50–50 for a single day. However, shares will often go up four or five days in a row, or will do the opposite. That is a great short-term indicator. The more consecutive days a share goes up or down, the higher the odds of it reversing, even if only for a few days.

Once you have determined you want to buy a particular company, don't wait until it goes up several days in a row. That is not a short-term indicator of strength; it is the opposite. You will want to buy after it has gone up a lot, but you can't invest in the past, only in the future.

Looking at the chart of Novo Resources, it will be obvious that there are dozens of times when you could have bought and sold for a 25 percent profit in a week. But wait, you say, I think Novo can go up 200 percent in a year and I want to capture that gain.

Work out the math. If you can capture a 25 percent move eight times in a year, you have made your 200 percent on the stock. If you were to measure all the up moves in Novo in a year and compare them to all of the down movement, Novo has probably moved 2,000 percent in a year.

If you really are reading this to make money (most people say they want to make money but then do the same stupid shit everyone else does), don't try to capture the 200 percent change. Instead, capture a lot of the ten or 15 percent gains. They happen far more often, and getting one-tenth of the total movement in Novo in a year is a lot more likely than getting a 200 percent move right.

You don't have to restrict yourself to only the $100 bills you may find lying on the ground. Pick up the nickels when you see them. There are far more of them.

I remember how in March of 2000 the Nasdaq seemed to go up day after day. There was no stopping it; it was going to the moon. In fact, the index climbed for 19 trading days in a row. Tell me that's not the greatest sentiment indicator of all time. All things change. If it goes up 19 days in a row, the next major move is down. The odds of anything going up or down that many times in a row are two to the 18th power. That happens about once in 20 lifetimes.

You must trade in an account where the gains are tax-free, such as an RRSP or IRA. I repeat that you should trade the appropriate symbol, not a derivative such as an OTCBB or a German symbol that is not the real stock. Buy after a number of days of decline. Sell after a number of days of advances. Remember, if a stock has gone up four or five or six days in a row, mathematically the chances are higher of a reverse with each day of similar movement.

Take a profit when you can, or you are going to take a loss when you have to.

Join the 5–15% group deliberately, because everyone else automatically joins the 85–95% club. Treat them nicely; they want to give all their money to you. Accept it gracefully, with a big smile.

Chapter 11
Investing in Odds and Sods in Energy

IF YOU WANT TO MAKE A SMALL FORTUNE, the fastest and easiest way is to find an absolutely no-lose deal in energy. Energy in all its various forms is by far the biggest business in the world today.

Here is how you pull it off. You find the very best story, something so bulletproof that it would take a blithering idiot working round the clock to screw it up. Find a fool who tells lies all the time. Then you invest a large fortune. . .

In 2002, uranium dropped to under $8 a pound and two fellows started an energy company to specialize in uranium and other energy minerals; one scalawag named Bill Henderson and another named Ralph Kettell. For contrarians, the timing was perfect. The price of uranium had been falling ever since the accident at Three Mile Island in March of 1979. It went from around $40 a pound to a low below $7 in 2001. If there was a commodity hated throughout the world in 2002, it would be U_3O_8.

The pair picked up an option on a uranium property called the Anderson Project, located 75 miles northwest of Phoenix. The claim block of nine square miles had been explored in the 1970s by the Minerals Exploration Corporation, to the point of completing a preliminary feasibility study in 1977, with plans for a mill with a capacity of 2,000 tons a day. The accident at Three Mile Island killed demand for uranium and Min Ex walked away from the project. Depending on the grade you use, the 1,400 holes drilled on those nine square miles during the 1970s defined up to 75 million pounds of U_3O_8.

The original deal between the partners called for Ralph Kettell to put up $50,000 in the corporation to get a 50 percent interest. Henderson, well worth a whole book all to himself on the subject of ethics in mining, wanted out of the company and would sell his half for $50,000. Kettell came to me and asked what I thought of the deal and the project. As it turned out, there was another rare earths and specialty metals property also owned by the company.

I listened to Kettell ramble on and on about what a great deal the Anderson property was. After all, it was the largest defined U_3O_8 resource in the United States. I suggested to Ralph that the project was a spreadsheet property. That confused him, as it should have done, because I had just made up the term on the spot.

I explained patiently. "Ralph," I began, "when you create a spreadsheet, you put the price of your commodity in the upper left corner of the sheet. Then you put in all your costs and assumptions, and in the lower right hand corner you have a number that represents either profit or loss, depending on your inputs and the initial price of the commodity. When the number gets high enough in that upper left box, eventually the value in the lower right goes positive."

Barbara, my wife and master, put in $10,000 to buy 10 percent of the company from Henderson. We did some advertising for Kettell and set up a website for him. Kettell bought the rest of the shares from Henderson. At one point we owned 13 percent of Concentric Energy, as it was named, and Ralph owned the remaining 87 percent.

Lo and behold, the ugly duckling started to grow up and got more beautiful with each passing day. Uranium prices hit $10 a pound, then $15, and kept going higher. We had timed the bottom perfectly. It went to $20, soon to $30 and then even higher, to $40 and $50 a pound.

Kettell was tracking Paladin Energy, a uranium company in Australia that had resources of exactly the same grade as Concentric, and twice as many pounds. It grew to a $100 million market cap, then $500 million and beyond, so it was easy to see what Concentric was worth. All we had to do was get a quote on Paladin, calculate its market cap and halve it.

Ralph began to pitch the company and the Anderson property to prospective investors. He found eager buyers. Even as a private company he managed to find about $21 million in funding. One hiccup turned out to be his ownership of so many shares. Investors realize that with a private concern, anyone holding over half the company can do pretty much whatever he wants. So Kettell parked a bunch of his shares with family members, with the agreement that when he wanted them back, they would sign them over.

He was also uncomfortable with Barbara owning over 10 percent, thinking ahead to when he went public, when all her trades would become public knowledge. He suggested we sell some shares to others so we could get below that 10 percent number. So Barbara came up with a list and gave three percent of the company away to family and friends. It was a nice thing to do, and if the company were ever to hit $100 million or more, those shares would be lifestyle-changing for the people she handed them to for free.

Ralph fell so naturally into the role of rich mining tycoon that he started to think and act the part. He took his wife on an expensive trip to a resort on the coast of Mexico. Excited by the adventure, and tiring after a few drinks over dinner, she begged off to return to their room to read a book. Ralph stayed in the bar for a nightcap, and a lovely lass slithered over next to him and began to talk. She was just fascinated by his vast experience in mining and finance. When he asked what her occupation was, she responded that she was a hooker from Argentina and just loved mining people.

Ralph smiled and asked if they could get together some time. That time came sooner than he thought, because when he and his wife returned home, she announced that she wanted to take a tour of England with the kids. Ralph smiled again and agreed the best thing she could do would be to take a week or ten days to wander around the UK. She took off for London; he took off for Buenos Aires.

Alas, one of the kiddies got sick at the airport, so she canceled her trip and returned to an empty house. Her trip was canceled, but his wasn't. Ralph's plans called for him to return to Baltimore just in time to make it home before the family's return from England. It's hard to say just who was the more surprised: him, at finding her home early, or her, finding him not home.

Ralph explained carefully to his wife and the mother of his children that he had been tied up with business in Argentina with his new girlfriend, who just happened to be a prostitute. "Look, here's her card. She even has her own website."

Readers of this book may be thinking that I have stepped over the line here in detailing Kettell's love life, but actually he was quite willing to tell everyone he knew, and their wives, about his girlfriend, the hooker. It wasn't as if she was fucking him for money. She really loved him.

That may have been the beginning of the end for Concentric, though we didn't realize it at the time. The quote for uranium kept going up and Ralph made plans to take the company public. His wife threw him out of the house and divorced him, but everyone was happy because Paladin Energy, the Australian lookalike, hit $500 million and then a billion.

Between the hooker expenses and the slightly illegal aspects of parking shares in the company, Kettell realized the best thing he could do would be to hand over the day-to-day running of the company to professional management, so he could pay proper attention to his new love.

Andy Simpson, a fellow from Northern California, took over the reins at Concentric with the sole goal of taking it public so everyone could cash in. By now Concentric had cream-of-the-crop investors from all of Canada and most of the US invested in the company, even if it was still private. It was the go-to uranium deal. All they had to do was get it public.

I believe I mentioned that if you want to make a small fortune, you need to put a large fortune into the hands of a fool who is also a giant liar. From 2003 until the very top of the market for uranium in 2007, near $136 a pound, Kettell maintained that the company would be public in ninety days. He said so throughout 2003 and 2004 and 2005 and 2006 and right into the very top in June of 2007.

What he didn't realize was that Andy Simpson was stealing the company blind. I was part of a group that later sued the company for fraud. Concentric Energy raised something like $21 million as a private company and spent near $18 million on everything but the deposit. In the entire existence of the company it carried out one 2,500-meter drill program. Even guys who are running a hobby resource company with no intention ever to do anything except create a lifestyle for themselves manage to complete bigger drill programs than that.

Andy Simpson had absolutely no intention of ever taking the company public. He couldn't allow it, as the disclosure requirements associated with doing so would have revealed how much money he was shoveling into his pockets. It would go public over his dead body. In the later legal disclosures Simpson claimed that he hadn't been taking his medicine for diabetes during the entire period he ran the company, and as a result he was stoned constantly.

The board of directors was just as bad. They sat and watched the company being raped. They said and did nothing except to collect directors' fees they were not entitled to, according to the agreement drawn up when the company was started. But if it was OK for the president of the company to steal, why should they not participate?

Uranium tanked in 2007 after blowing up in a bubble. The company never went public. The Australian lookalike peaked at well over $2 billion, its stock price going from $.89 in April of 2005 to a high of $8.71 in March of 2007. Concentric was doing placements at $8 in 2005, so if it had continued tracking Paladin Energy, it would have been an $80 stock when it went public. But it never went public.

That was hardly the end of the stupidity on the part of Ralph Kettell. He spun off the other Nevada-based energy metals project that I mentioned to the Concentric shareholders. It had over $15 million worth of exploration done on it during the 1970s and he had all the documentation from that work. When he divorced he somehow tossed $15 million worth of exploration data in the trash. When specialty metals and rare earths took off in price in 2010, that spinoff company would also have been worth over $1 billion, had it been a public company.

And to Ralph's giant surprise, when uranium tanked the hooker from Argentina dumped him. Maybe it wasn't true love after all.

My next adventure in energy investment was to put money into a convertible debenture of a small Canadian oil field operator. The fellow who convinced me to invest in the deal was the vice president of a silver company that I had given a lot of help. He had previously been a stockbroker, and that should have been a sufficient warning to me.

Oil peaked at $135 a barrel in June of 2008, then started down as all commodities tanked going into the GFC, the Global Financial Crisis. I asked my friend, who was chairman of the board, if there was any price at which the company would be hurt. I probably asked fifty times, and was assured fifty times there was zero danger to the price of the stock.

When a former stockbroker uses the term "zero danger" he really means maximum danger, and you should get out at once. I didn't, and the company went bankrupt. The debenture holders had a claim on the assets of the company, but all the same my money was tied up for six months until the finances were straightened out. Late 2008 and early 2009 was one of those wonderful once-in-a-lifetime opportunities to invest in resources. I couldn't, because I had believed in a former broker and all my spare money was tied up in the bankruptcy court.

Since I hadn't gotten whacked enough times to understand what was going on in the energy field, someone then convinced me to look at a coal bed methane (CBM) company based in Indonesia.

Indonesia used to be a member of OPEC but its declining production eventually meant the country had to conserve its oil production for domestic consumption. It withdrew from OPEC and focused on rationalizing its energy production.

Some bright spark in the government realized that while Indonesia had an oil ministry that controlled oil production, and a natural gas ministry, and a ministry to govern coal production, it had no Coal Bed Methane Department.

You could drill for oil, with the right permits. You could drill for natural gas if you filled out all the forms and got permission, and you could mine coal. But since there was no CBM division, you couldn't drill for or produce coal bed methane. Yet under the right geological conditions, coal beds may still contain the methane gas they once produced.

The government of Indonesia realized it was missing out on a great opportunity to tax CBM production. It opened the country to applications from companies wanting to drill for and produce CBM.

Some Canadians floated a company they named CBM Asia. Great name, by the way. They raised some money and applied for some coal fields on an island with an LNG plant nearby. They got permission to drill and began a work program.

Coal is interesting because in using it as fuel, you lose all the CBM because it will escape into the atmosphere, if it still exists. But if you have a coal bed with water overlying it, sealing the seams of coal, the CBM may well have remained in place, ready for exploitation. And since coal is often found in flat seams of material, in some fields you can drill on 500-meter centers and still be in the measured category because the bed is so predictable.

This means that a company drilling for CBM doesn't have to do very much drilling to define an economic deposit. So CBM Asia began to drill. It released its first results and disappointed the market. There was barely any gas in the coal. That didn't make any sense to me because there had been a hole drilled nearby with great results. How was it possible for one company to drill and report bonanza results, and another company drills the same bed of coal and gets nothing?

I asked the guy running the company a lot of probing questions and finally got him to 'fess up. They hadn't bothered to send a geologist out to supervise the drilling. All the drill crew knew was that they were to drill a coal seam at a specified location. They did that. They hit the coal seam exactly where they expected it to be, and put the coal into drill core boxes just as they had done dozens of times before. What the drill crew didn't realize until they handed over the coal intercept to CBM Asia was that they were supposed to have bagged the coal to seal it, so the gas content could be measured. No one had told them to do that.

So CBM Asia had a coal intercept showing no CBM. They continued drilling after showing the drill crew how to bag the core for testing. The rest of the gas results from the drill program were excellent and could be used for the 51-101 resource report. However, they had to include the meaningless numbers from the first hole. That made all of their resource numbers look a lot worse than they were.

Time went on and management got dumber. Rather than actually produce, which had been the plan all along, the president of the company concentrated on picking up more and more land positions. He was burning through cash like a drunken sailor on Saturday night but the company now controlled a lot of land. While he was busy going into the real estate business, the price of CBM hovered around $12 per million cubic feet, or MMCF. They had economic holes and they were conveniently near an LNG plant, but rather than produce and conserve cash, they went on a land spree. Then a former partner sued them.

Remember, this was Indonesia. If a local decides for whatever reason to sue a Canadian company, the Canadian company loses. Indonesia is one of the most corrupt countries on earth. The president of the company assured me a dozen times it was meaningless. They had retained a local high-priced lawyer who was connected and they weren't going to lose.

They lost.

They had pissed away all their free cash on land purchases. Since their 51-101 was so poor due to their not having bagged the core, and with the president of the company unwilling to come clean with the market, the company went bankrupt.

If you find a company with a story so compelling, so bulletproof that it simply cannot fail, rest assured that the village idiot is right around the corner looking for a job. When you believe it would work even if someone spent twenty-four hours a day, seven days a week trying to screw it up, you will find that the village idiot ends up running the company and puts in a lot of overtime.

I discovered another fool and liar when I began to cover a tiny oil production company based in north Texas named Molori Energy, run by Joel Dumaresq. Joel presented the company to me as partnering with another, larger company to rework existing wells that needed upgrades. The cost to rework the wells was low and they provided an immediate increase in cash flow.

"And by the way," he said, "we are looking at drilling some shallow wells and fracking a zone that has been ignored by everyone. But a neighborhood producer has been drilling and fracking the zone for a cost of $300,000 a well and getting an average of fifty-five barrels a day in each well."

Here's how the math worked, or at least here's what I was told. A shallow well cost $250,000 to $300,000 to drill and complete. A flowing barrel of oil was worth $60,000 in a deal. So they invest $300,000 and do an average 55 BOEPD well that is now worth $3.3 million to the company.

The four deadliest words in investing are, "This time it's different." But whenever the president of a company says, "And by the way," that's right up there on the Richter scale. Maybe I should add it to Chapter 3.

They had a great plan that was working when they did the recompletions. Why screw around with a good plan?

But it got worse. Since Molori controlled only 30 percent of the projects, it had to allow its partner to make all the decisions as to when and where to drill. Molori had the money in the bank to drill, but apparently the partner kept coming up with excuses for not drilling.

They were in the oil business. In the oil business, it's drill and produce or die.

As time went on I was told more and more about the shallow drilling into the previously ignored oil structure. Dumaresq began talking about wanting to do deals around the company's basic land position. The planned well got postponed and then postponed again. Nothing was ever reported about even a single recompletion. It seemed to me that the story changed right under my nose.

Finally Molori did another deal with its original partner and now controlled the entire field by itself. That thrilled me because now there would be no more excuses for a lack of progress on the drilling front. Actually, there were more excuses. It finally turned out that the delays were caused not by the now former partner but by Molori. Dumaresq feared other companies glomming on to his key to success, so he didn't really want to drill in case someone else figured it out.

So, in well over a year of dealing with an oil exploration company, Molori managed to drill two shallow wells. The results were so pitiful that Dumaresq refused to tell the market what the final flow figures were. And he kept doing deals, picking up more land. Each time he was promising to pay money the company didn't have. The oil price dropped. Then he sued his former partner. That is almost always news the market is eager to hear. Molori tanked, and by every measure the company is bankrupt.

In one of the many discussions I had with Dumaresq I suggested that all he had to do was drill off the thousand or so drill locations he already controlled and he would have a billion-dollar company. But he wanted more. He kept doing deals and spending money he didn't have and couldn't raise. I wanted Molori to be an oil exploration and development company; Joel Dumaresq turned it into a real estate company on the sly and blew his shareholders out of the water.

No matter what the company is and how wonderful things look, when you figure out that the guy running it cannot tell the truth, bail out.

I have lost more money listening to liars than market conditions ever cost me. There are some people who seem incapable of telling the truth. They will lie to your face, knowing you will figure it out ten minutes later. And they still insist on lying.

I don't mind making a mistake. As an investor in junior resource stocks you will make lots of mistakes in the hope of finding that one great company that more than makes up for all the duds. But listening to liars gets very expensive.

Chapter 12
Investing in the Rest of the Pack

THE BIGGEST INDUSTRIES in the resource sector tend to be controlled by major companies. The coal industry, iron, phosphate mining and oil are pretty much dominated by big companies. Investing in them is more a function of the state of the market than based on financial numbers. In 2008 coal and oil and iron all tanked, and no matter how well run the company was, its share price dropped. As commodity prices recovered, so did share prices. It had everything to do with the market and next to nothing to do with the companies.

For gains in the hundreds of percent — the lifestyle-changing price gains — you have to play in the junior mining sand pit. It's hard to do, for there is little real data about the companies. Their managements tell lies all the time and few juniors are run as serious businesses. I have said for years that people in mining are very smart and mostly overeducated. By and large they would have far more success if they worked at a 7-11 for a semester and learned how to sell a quart of milk at a profit.

Energy seems to offer a compelling range of opportunities for profit, but the industry attracts guys like Ralph Kettell, who was on an ego trip to show everyone how smart he was and blew up Concentric Energy. Al Charuk, who ran CBM Asia kicking and screaming into bankruptcy, had ambitions far bigger than his grasp. He had perfect timing but didn't pay attention to detail. He made error after error and just hoped investors wouldn't notice. Joel Dumaresq took a great idea and tried to make it into something far bigger than his bandwidth would support. If you don't know how to sell a quart of milk at a profit, running an energy deal is probably the wrong business for you.

In the real junior mining sector, a management that is fast on its feet and capable of telling people what they want to hear can make a career of doing little more than raising money, drilling, raising money and drilling, until retirement kicks in. When the market is favorable they do a pump and dump. When the market sucks due to an absence of progress and the shares hit new lows, they hand themselves a bucket filled with options because they have done such a sterling job of running the venture.

But do not confuse a lack of progress with a lack of investment opportunity. From 1999 to 2001, cash was selling at a big discount in the gold and silver markets. I saw silver projects being given away in Mexico to anyone willing to take them over on a non-recourse basis. If you could make the project work, you kept the profit. If you failed, you could walk away and it wouldn't cost you anything.

After every dawn comes the light. From 2001 to 2005 or so, you could invest in the biggest turkey and watch it fly as if it was aimed at heaven. Again, after the GFC in 2008, from 2009 until 2011 every resource company run by someone with a heartbeat doubled or tripled. After the major bottom in late 2015 and early 2016, the share prices of many juniors again made gains of hundreds of percent.

What I'm trying to say is that investing in juniors and making a profit has far more to do with timing than with the commodity, the management, or country risk. Those factors are all interesting but the phase of the investment cycle as measured by sentiment is far more important.

I presume there are few 12-year-olds reading this book, even if it would be advantageous for them to know what's in it. Since we are all adults, then, I can say some things the snowflakes might have a problem with. Most people, including investors, are dumber than bricks. They run from one stupid idea right into another. We had the dot-com stock market boom in 2000. In March of 2000 I read something on the web about how inmates in a jail in Baltimore were holding stock picking contests. You know you have run out of fools looking to invest when crack dealers begin to discuss the merits of putting money into a stock market bubble.

After that, in 2006–08, we had the peak in the real estate bubble when even your cat could qualify for a no-doc loan to buy a house. Brokers then took bundles of the sub-prime used toilet paper carrying AAA ratings and peddled them to hedge funds eager to chase yield, no matter what the risk. That blew up and nearly took the entire worldwide financial system with it.

In 2017 the flock of sheep that is most investors ran into the Bitcon swindle and threw money at over 2,500 varieties of electronic Beanie Babies, all based on them having a high valuation because of their supposed rarity. That particular mass delusion has cost the idiots who jumped in to capture the top an 80 percent loss so far. And people still talk about Bitcon as if it were a real commodity with a real value. It is not.

Lately, marijuana in all its variations seems to have caught the attention of the herd. I think you can see where I am going. People invest in the same way sheep munch grass in a farmer's field. They munch away peacefully until one of them gets it into her head to panic. All of a sudden the entire troop heads off in whatever direction the leader points them, without a single thought in those tiny little brains as to where they are going, or why. People invest in exactly the same way, and they too will eventually be sheared and eaten.

The Internet is the most valuable information tool ever invented. Ordinary people have access to more data and valuable advice than at any time in recorded history. In 1929 Joseph Kennedy and Bernard Baruch may have had inside information about the coming stock market crash, but Joe Six-Pack had no clue.

Today everyone has instant access to accurate and quite valuable material. The wise investor must still determine the difference between signal and noise. There are a lot of wolves out there looking for an easy kill.

I think I have presented a lot of new information and ideas that would help an investor of any experience to make better investing decisions. Given the incredibly dangerous state of the world's financial system, it may be time to reconsider just how you invest, so as to protect your family and your money.

Chapter 13
Helpful Hints

1. Guns don't kill people. Margin does. Those who invest using margin want to hand you all their money, and in time they will. If you feel rotten about taking it, don't. I'll take it and not feel a bit rotten. If you use margin, eventually the margin clerk will be on the phone and he's not a nice person.

2. Failure is the standard in resources and is the rule, not the exception. Take a profit when you can and move on.

3. Narrative follows price. A lot of price movement is little more than random noise. No matter what a market does, most people want to explain it with whatever the news of the day is. It's random. The price happens first and then people try to justify it.

4. Lightning rarely strikes twice in the same place. If a company reports wonderful results and can't back up those results with further progress, bail.

5. Buy on the cannons, sell on the trumpets.

6. The managements of many resource companies are there to collect pay checks for as long as investors will put up with them. You can think of them as lifestyle companies. When you notice that the guys running the company have confused motion with action, look for a better home for your capital.

7. Investors are naturally biased to be buyers rather than sellers. Mathematically, something can go infinitely higher but can go down by no more than 100 percent. So shares will actually go down more often than they go up. Smart short sellers can make a lot of money betting against the crowd. At the right time, naturally.

8. In a boring market a company's positive news release may only provide a liquidity event rather than propelling its share price higher. Liquidity is your friend. Learn to love it.

9. If you think buying physical metals from the cheapest dealer makes sense, you may want to understand that the likelihood of that dealer going belly up is the

highest. When buying physical metals, if the dealer can't deliver right now, don't buy. Metals dealers go bust all the time.

10. You can never invest in the past, only the future. A hockey player once said, "Skate to where the puck is going to be, not where it is." Markets turn all the time and signal those turns in advance. Skate to where the market is going to be, not where it was. You can't drive well looking at your rear view mirror.

11. For the last couple of years the junior resource companies have tended to make a high in mid-year and at year-end. It makes sense for stocks to recover after the tax-loss silly season but I can't really explain the mid-year high. In any case it's worth following the seasonality charts.

12. When the markets open, the first 30 minutes is often controlled by emotional buying from the crowd eager to get into a position. Lows for the day often happen between noon and 2pm, when the brokers are all out of the office, sipping their first drinks of the day. The smart money does its buying and selling at the end of the trading session. Many times you will see bigger moves in the final few minutes of trading, in either direction.

13. Everything you read, hear or watch is some combination of signal and noise. If you follow someone because you agree with 100 percent of what he says, it's probably noise. All he is doing is telling you what you want to hear. Gurus are 99 percent noise, experts are 90 percent noise, and Internet chatboards give the clueless an opportunity to show how smart they are by saying everyone else is stupid. Ignore the trolls.

14. Good news travels on an airplane. Bad news rides in on a donkey. When drill results seem to take months longer than they should, almost always they are poor, and management is hoping investors have forgotten about the planned drill program.

15. If nothing else at all has changed except the price, consider averaging down your cost. If the car of your dreams sells for $40,000 and the dealer lowers the price to $20,000 in a sale, it's a good deal. Stocks work the same way. You don't wait until milk has gone up five days in a row to buy, so why would you do so with stocks?

16. The greatest sentiment indicator — only rarely found — is when the stock

market discounts the cash a company has in the till. From 1999 to 2001 and again in 2008 there were dozens of resource juniors selling for a fraction of the cash they had in the bank. When you see that happening, buy the companies with the greatest discount. Every night before you go to bed, get on your knees and pray that the president of the company gets charged with being a paedophile and the company shuts down. There is more than one way to skin a cat.

17. Never confuse brains with a bull market. There is a big difference. The day you think you are as smart as the market, the market will kick your butt.

18. Plain old cash is an investment. Much of the time in resources it may be the best thing you can invest in.

Chapter 14
Tools I Use

WHILE I HAVE ATTEMPTED to give readers some of what I think are the most important basics of investing, obviously you have to use other tools to get information.

I'm going to give readers a list of some of the sites I use to find information. I have no relationship with them whereby I get paid, so it doesn't matter to me financially if you sign up with them or not. These are just people I know and like — like a lot, in some cases.

1. At 321gold.com we provide our readers with a wide variety of opinions from both paid and free sites. I can't list every site and writer that I like and use, as I do this 8–10 hours a day and cover a lot of territory. We will post any reasonable opinion, no matter if we agree with it or not. There is a lot of parroting on gold sites. You see the same rubbish posted again and again without a vestige of either logic or fact included. If it's not either factual or logical, we won't post it.

2. The best source of free information on the web for current metals prices is Kitco.com. Everyone uses them. We link to their site for our price data.

3. For up-to-the-minute quotes on Canadian and US stocks, you might try StockWatch.com or StockHouse.com. They both offer a lot of free information and have some paid services. I use Stockwatch constantly and pay about $12 a month.

4. If you want to really make money, you have to understand and use the bullish consensus numbers. My favorite is the Daily Sentiment Index, edited and composed by the brilliant Jake Bernstein. The website is located at secure.trade-futures.com. I also follow consensus-inc.com. They provide weekly readings on 32 commodity markets and offer a one-week free trial.

    Market Vane offers a similar service that costs $25 a month for daily updates and $45 a month for weekly updates. They are at MarketVane.net. If you can pick one top or bottom in any market using nothing but bullish consensus, you will have paid for more than ten years of any of these services.

runs Dollar Collapse. He is one of the best speakers and most
ble people I listen to. The site is free and loaded with good
. When you listen to him you will learn a lot that you hadn't
. He's brilliant.

rb Steve Saville runs The Speculative Investor. He provides two
repo. ach week covering the stock market, commodities, bonds, currencies
and precious metals. He understands how and why the markets work as well
as or better than anyone else I know. His site can be found at speculative-
investor.com. Whenever there is an issue of bad or poor information becoming
commonly accepted, Steve does a wonderful job of explaining how and why a
particular market functions as opposed to how the herd believes it functions.
The subscription cost of $25 monthly or $240 a year seems pretty cheap.

7. Tom McClellan puts out the McClellan Market Report at $195 a year and The
   Daily Edition at $600 a year. Like Bob Hoye (see below), the research and
   timing is magnificent and well worth the price. There's a 14-day free trial offer
   for new subscribers at Mcoscillator.com. The market reports are published
   approximately monthly.

8. One of the finest minds and best writers can be found for free on our site, on
   Fridays. Adam Hamilton's site is called Zealllc.com. The service costs $119
   yearly and is cheap at half the price. In April of 2011 he was one of the very
   few calling a top in silver. In December of 2015 he nailed the bottom in gold
   and silver. He is neither a guru nor an expert. He just calls them as he sees
   them, with great accuracy.

9. In my view the single best writer on the web writing about things financial
   would be Grant Williams of Things That Make You Go Hmmm... Ttmygh.com.
   He charges $295 for a one-year subscription. I've always felt the best all round
   writer of the last 50 years was Richard Russell, but he left us in 2015. Grant is
   just as good. Send him an email at info@ttmygh.com and request a trial
   subscription. It's well worth it. I just don't know how he writes so much, so
   well. I couldn't do it.

10. Bob Hoye of Institutional Advisors has one of the finest and most accurate
    subscription services on the web at institutionaladvisors.com. The service is
    aimed at high net worth individuals and portfolio managers. He is very good.
    For a free 30-day trial, email r.brian.ripley@gmail.com. The service is not

cheap but if you want the best in anything, you have to pay for it. Except for me. I'm free.

11. Here is another very valuable service for those who need a feel for the market and what is going on. RealVisionTV.com delivers 150 interviews a year with the greatest names in finance for $364 (less than a dollar a day). They offer a free one-week trial.

12. Maurice Jackson of Proven and Probable does a great job of interviewing people from all over the mining space. The site is free and a good source of information. Good questions make good interviews. provenandprobable.com

13. Robert Sinn runs another educational free website specializing in things about mining and economics. Somehow he manages to interview me on the occasional time I get it dead right. I won't take all the credit, everyone honest makes bad calls all the time and I am no exception. He makes a lot of great calls. energyandgold.com/

14. I'm coming around to the opinion that all investors, including me, tend to overthink investment decisions. I've been watching James Flanagan of Gann Global Financial. He has been nailing market tops and bottoms for years. His work showed me that while the vast majority of commentators on the metals tend to zoom in and micro analyze every twist and turn in gold and silver, actually all the metals have been doing since 2011 is tracking all the other commodities. You didn't have to worry about what was happening with gold, as sugar and coffee were doing exactly the same thing. GannGlobal.com is probably worth looking at closely. James offers a free trial and a variety of different packages. I recommend him highly. He is not a gold or silver guy, he covers everything.

15. The single best site for paid charts and data of anything metals-related has to be Nick Laird of goldchartsrus.com. He charges $200 for a year's subscription. If you don't know if you need his service or not, he will give you a three-week trial for $10. If you want to trade the gold/silver ratio or platinum/gold spread, his site is invaluable. He can be reached at nick@goldchartsrus.com.

You are allowed to think for yourself. There are a lot of people who don't want you thinking for yourself. Investing is not rocket science but it does require intelligent questions if you want to get the right answers.

Appendix
Links to Articles

Pages 29 to 35; gold price forecasts in 2011
    http://www.munknee.com/is-gold-on-its-way-to-3000-5000-10000-or-even-higher-these-analysts-think-so/

Page 38; S&P 500 year-end predictions
    https://realinvestmentadvice.com/the-problem-with-wall-streets-forecasts/

Page 47; *Sentiment indicates extremes of emotion for lots of commodities*
    https://www.streetwisereports.com/article/2018/01/25/sentiment-indicates-extremes-of-emotion-for-lots-of-commodities.html

Page 47; Jake Bernstein's DSI service
    https://www.netpressinc.com/store/product/daily-sentiment-index-dsi-1-yr/

Page 48; *Sentiment Says, Turn, Turn, Turn*
    http://www.321gold.com/editorials/moriarty/moriarty122418.html

Page 51; *Facts on Silver*
    http://www.321gold.com/editorials/moriarty/moriarty042511.html

Pages 72 to 77; investing in royalty stocks
    https://www.fool.com/investing/2018/05/13/these-gold-streaming-stocks-are-buys-for-2018.aspx

Pages 81 to 85; metals ETFs
    https://www.investopedia.com/articles/etfs-mutual-funds/062416/top-5-precious-metal-etfs.asp

Pages 85 to 87; gold mutual funds
    http://www.goldbullionpro.com/top-10-gold-mutual-funds/

Printed in Great Britain
by Amazon

44054371R00059